Irvine Welsh's
Trainspotting

CONTINUUM CONTEMPORARIES

Also available in this series

Forthcoming in this series

· **IRVINE WELSH'S**

Trainspotting

A READER'S GUIDE

ROBERT MORACE

CONTINUUM | NEW YORK | LONDON

For Robin and Arun Neal

2001

The Continuum International Publishing Group Inc
370 Lexington Avenue, New York, NY 10017

The Continuum Intrernational Publishing Group Ltd
The Tower Building, 11 York Road, London SE1 7NX

www.continuumbooks.com

Printed in the United States of America

Library of Congress Cataloging-in-Publication Data

Morace, Robert A.
  Irvine Welsh's Trainspotting : a reader's guide / Robert Morace.
      p. cm.— (Continuum contemporaries)
  Includes bibliographical references.
ISBN 0-8264-5237-X
    1. Welsh, Irvine. Trainspotting. 2. Edinburgh (Scotland)—In literature. 3.
Narcotic habit in literature. 4. Young men in literature. I. Title. II. Series.

PR6073.E47 T736 2001
823'.914—dc21   2001032337

Contents

The Novelist

Even in an age of promiscuous praise and fleeting fame, the litany of honorifics bestowed upon the author of "the junkie bible" is impressive as well as instructive: Scottish William Burroughs, wild man of literature, most vital of contemporary authors, leader of a cultural renaissance, maker of the British Buzz, savior of British literature, national monument, and poet laureate of the chemical generation. What makes the list all the more startling, especially for someone who grew up associating writing with graffiti, is that writing was something Irvine Welsh "just stumbled into" (McGavin, 1996). Even after he had begun writing, he did not think that anyone would actually publish his work, or that it would ever attract a wide and surprisingly diversified as well as dedicated following. Even when it did, he refused to define himself as a writer. "I just feel like someone who's written something," he explained just a few months after *Trainspotting*'s release ("It's Generational and Geographical," 1994). Thirteen months later, the book's and his own success now assured, he made much the same point, one that is crucial to an accurate understanding and appreciation of the "Irvine Welsh phenomenon": "I'm just someone who's written something and might write something else if I've got anything to say" (Mulholland, 1995). Which of course he did.

Irvine Welsh was born in 1961 in Leith, the economically depressed port area of Edinburgh, just north of the Scottish capital's flourishing city center. (Originally a separate municipality, Leith became part of Edinburgh in 1920.) When he was four, his family moved from working class Leith to Muirhouse, taking up residence in one of those characterless, depressingly modern housing estates ("schemes" in British slang, equivalent to "housing projects" in the United States) erected during the early postwar period. It was an experiment in social engineering — modernism for the masses — that would have disastrous consequences in cities throughout the UK and the United States, undermining community while breeding the boredom, hopelessness, and individual social pathologies that Lynne Ramsay captures so well in her 1999 film, *Ratcatcher*, set in Glasgow during the 1973 refuse collectors' strike. Welsh's father had worked on Leith's docks until ill health forced him to take up less strenuous employment as a carpet salesman; Welsh's mother waited tables. Welsh, meanwhile, attended local schools. Despite interests in English and art, he left Ainslee Park Secondary School when he was sixteen. After completing a City Guild course in electrical engineering, he worked as a television repairman until he was literally shocked (electrically that is) into taking up a succession of less risky menial jobs before leaving Edinburgh for London in 1978 to pursue his interest in punk music. In London, Welsh occupied various squats and bedsits, experimented with drugs, got into trouble in a small but persistent way, and sang and played guitar in the bands The Pubic Lice and Stairway 13. He spent his twenties drifting between London and Edinburgh, between "crap jobs" and the dole.

When a series of arrests for petty crimes culminated in a suspended sentence for trashing a North London community center, a shaken Welsh decided to clean up his act, one which he had fueled with copious amounts of alcohol and lesser quantities of speed and (briefly) heroin. He worked as a clerk for the Hackney Council (London) and studied computing under a grant from the Manpower Services Commission. In the mid-1980s, the post-punk Welsh turned budding entrepreneur, taking advantage of the London housing boom by buying, renovating, and selling bedsits in Hackney, Islington, and Camden. Returning to Edinburgh in the late 1980s, Welsh found employment as a training officer in the city's housing department, ironically enough, the very department that had planned the Muirhouse housing estates. No less ironically, the former punk and whilom yuppie did well in his job, earning promotions and the opportunity to study for an MBA at Heriot-Watt University. Welsh proved a good student even though he found the program unchallenging. He wrote a thesis on using training to create equal opportunities for women which his advisor judged "persuasive" in all respects but one: the writing, he said, just "wasn't very forceful" (Beckett, 1998).

The MBA program might have pointed Welsh down the yellow brick road of middle class respectability (he started a consultancy firm in order to supplement his income) had it not also given the bored student (and office worker) time to start writing fiction. Welsh had taken to writing to counteract boredom once before, during a Greyhound bus trip across the United States in the mid-1980s. Then he jotted down observations. Now he wrote about something that had become painfully clear to him since his return from London, something he had in fact begun noticing during those earlier

visits to his native city: the widespread use of heroin among people
he had known in Leith and Muirhouse, some of them already dead
from overdoses and AIDS-related causes, others HIV-positive,
mainly as a result of sharing needles. As Welsh pointed out shortly
after *Trainspotting* was published, "I began the book as a way of
trying to figure out the puzzles of drug dependency and the explo-
sion of HIV in Edinburgh" (Grant, 1993). By this time, Welsh was
well into the rave scene and writing, he noted, also helped him
"cope with the comedown phase after the frenzied high of the
weekend" (Reynolds, 1998). Multiply motivated, Welsh wrote
Trainspotting "in rapid but intermittent bursts over a two year period" (Grant, 1993).

Parts of *Trainspotting* began appearing in 1991 in the London-
based, decidedly low-budget *DOG* and more importantly in Glasgow's *West Coast Magazine*, and *Scream, If You Want to Go Faster:
New Writing Scotland No. 9*, edited by Hamish Whyte and Janice
Galloway. That same year, Edinburgh writer Duncan McLean, who
had founded Clocktower Press in 1990, was asked to run a writers'
workshop in Muirhouse. The following year, one of the group,
Kevin Williamson, started the magazine *Rebel Inc*, which would
publish parts of *Trainspotting* as well as Williamson's notorious
drug-fueled interview with Welsh. McLean, meanwhile, published
additional parts in two Clocktower pamphlets: *A Parcel of Rogues*
(which also included work by Galloway, James Kelman, Gordon
Legge and others) and *Past Tense: Four Stories from a Novel* ("our
slowest seller," McLean later joked). McLean was also instrumental
in Welsh's reaching a larger audience, beyond the readership of the
alternative literary magazines, small presses, and *Scream*, by recom-
mending Welsh to Robin Robertson, a Scot who was editorial director of Secker & Warburg (before moving to Jonathan Cape), which
had published McLean's collection of stories, *Bucket of Tongues* in
1992. Robertson, himself a fine poet and an ardent supporter of

new Scottish writing, decided to publish *Trainspotting* even though he thought it had little chance of selling well. Welsh, remember, never thought his book would be published in the first place. Both, of course, were wrong.

At the end of the tongue-in-cheek author's note to the 1993 Secker & Warburg edition of *Trainspotting*, Welsh is described (or more likely describes himself) as "at present working on a second novel and a collection of short stories." The collection became *The Acid House*; the second novel was a continuation of *Trainspotting* that he dropped because "I was sick of the characters by that time and decided that I wanted to write something fresh" (Welsh, "Introduction," *Acid*, vii). (Robertson would later offer a different account; presumably speaking of this same second novel, he said that he had rejected "The Chill-Out Zone" in 1994 because it was not very good, though parts were salvaged and later recycled in *Ecstasy: Three Novellas* [Beckett, 1998]). *Trainspotting* was published in 1993 (as was an alternative Visitor's Guide which Welsh co-wrote with Williamson and launched at that year's Edinburgh Book Festival) and nominated for the Booker Prize. It did not make the shortlist, however. As the jury's chairperson, Lord Gowrie, later reported, the three male judges were "too gentlemanly" to override the objections of the two female judges whose "feminist sensibilities" Welsh had offended (Porlock, 1996). *Trainspotting* failed to win the Whitbread first novel prize for a similar reason; one of the three judges found it offensive and got another to agree with him and award the prize to Rachel Cusk for *Saving Agnes* (Johnson, 1998). Not that not making the shortlist and not winning the Whitbread seemed to matter as *Trainspotting* made its way from relative obscurity to international renown, and notoriety. Undervalued and underestimated by the literary prize committees, Welsh's novel was receiving good, even enthusiastic notices in the popular press and the literary reviews and, equally important, word was spreading among British youth who could soon read more of Welsh's work in fashionable publications such as *Face*. Meanwhile, Harry Gibson's stage adaptation premiered in April 1994 as part of the Glasgow Mayfest, before being staged at the Edinburgh Fringe and in London (twice) before going on national tour. *Trainspotting* and its author were well on their way to becoming facts of British cultural life, and Welsh, in August 1995, was able to give up his day job at the Edinburgh Housing Department.

Much of the Welsh biography presented up to this point became known only after what has come to be called "the Irvine Welsh myth" had taken hold and the success of *Trainspotting* and *The Acid House* had led some of Welsh's less admiring critics to question whether the author was quite what he claimed, or others claimed him, to be: "a pure writer, an enfant sauvage, a literary Kasper Hauser, raised in darkness, schooled in depravity, unread, unlettered and unlearned but capable, given pen and paper, of producing staggering feats of storytelling," as Andy Beckett mimicked, not out of malice but in one of the earliest and best efforts to set the record straight. Others were more determined in their debunking of a myth they believed this self-proclaimed "literary equivalent of the football casuals" may well have started and at the very least had aided and abetted.

There is certainly—even appropriately given his Edinburgh background—a Dr. Jekyll and Mr. Hyde-like quality to Welsh, one that has in some ways grown more pronounced in the later work where the sensational and the sentimental are so jarringly juxtaposed. In interviews, the person whom McLean recalls as always dressed in shirt and tie comes across as either drunk and drugged or amiable and articulate, sometimes both at once: "a skinny, unhealthy-looking 37-year old with a round, battered face like a dissolute cherub's" and dressed not in the shirt and tie that McLean remembers but "a raver's uniform—brutally cropped hair, a scruffy brown jacket, T-shirt, faded jeans" yet "intellectually serious, speaking not in Edinburgh dialect but in educated Scots. Even to his friends, Welsh is an enigma" (Downer, 1996). And, like his character Mark Renton, something of an autodidact, at times speaking knowledgeably about books while at others claiming that his knowledge of, say, William Burroughs, Brendan Behan, and Dermot Bolger is entirely second-hand, via the songs of Iggy Pop, Lou Reed and the Pogues. The press played up the Mr. Hyde side, duly noting every arrest for being drunk and disorderly and instance of boorish behavior. At the same time, the press took no less delight in puncturing the myth it had helped create and continued to perpetuate, duly noting every time Welsh was guilty of turning his street cred into a nest egg, engaging in real estate speculation, owning residences in London, Amsterdam and Edinburgh (the last purchased for £L159,000, the shocked press reported). That he should leave the HIV capital of Europe to live and rave in drug-friendly Amsterdam nicely fit the press's image of the poet laureate of the chemical generation, but that he should go with his wife (that he should have a wife, an English one at that, about whom the usually voluble Welsh has been uncharacteristically reticent, arguably protective) was no less shocking. It was also useful to those who wished to prove that Welsh was not who he pretended to be — was, in fact, more the self-promoting entrepreneur than the post-punk generational spokesperson. There was even much ado in the mid-1990s about which generation Welsh belonged to as the artist formerly known as being thirty seven was reported to be a closet forty four year old.

Even as the *Observer* prepared for the February 1996 release of the film version of *Trainspotting* by gleefully unmasking "the wild man of literature" as a Jekyll-and-Hyde at best, a fraud at worst (McKay, 1996), another problem surfaced. The success of *Trainspotting* had ensured that each of Welsh's subsequent works received broader coverage, but even as they were being more widely reviewed they were being less enthusiastically received, as critics took note of the increasing splattershock sensationalism and the waning artistry. Jenny Turner, who had written the most perceptive and influential of the early reviews of *Trainspotting*, published in the *London Review of Books*, was highly critical of the later works. "There had been bad bits even in the magnificent *Trainspotting*. . . . But the good bits are so brilliant, you want to forgive him everything." Forgive him then, not now: "*Ecstasy* is the worst book yet from a writer who has been going from weakness to weakness ever since *Trainspotting* began its roll in 1993." Had success and sudden fame spoiled Irvine Welsh? Perhaps. Magazine editors, anthologists, and his own publisher asked for more of his work and more often than not he obliged, as he did in rushing *Ecstasy* into print so that its release would coincide with that of the film version of *Trainspotting*.

By mid-1996, the critical reaction to Welsh began looking like a full-scale backlash; the culture (or cultures: British, youth, consumer) was overdosing on an overexposed and seemingly omnipresent Welsh. All four of his books were on the bestseller list (simultaneously), two adaptations (*Trainspotting* and *Marabou Stork Nightmares*) were on stage, another on the screen; there was also a song, "The Big Man and the Scream Team Meet the Barmy Army," recorded with Primal Scream for the England-Scotland football match held at Wembley Stadium on June 15, 1996, plus all those anthologies featuring Welsh, everything from the staidly titled *The Picador Book of Contemporary Scottish Fiction* to *Acid Plaid*, *Ahead of Its Time*, *Artificial Paradises*, *A Book of Two Halves* and *Disco Biscuits*. *Ecstasy*, with its colorful and gleefully shocking, *Rebel, Inc*-inspired cover was released amidst the moral panic over the Ecstasy death of solidly middle class teen Leah Betts. Just as Welsh was, as part of the buildup to the film *Trainspotting*'s release in the United States in July 1996, being introduced to American readers of the

New York Times Magazine as "the undisputed star" of the new generation of Scottish writers (Downer, 1996), others in the UK were writing Welsh off. In the *Scotsman*, for example, conservative columnist (and novelist) Allan Massie made this very point, enlisting that "much respected pillar of Glasgow University's English Department," Professor Philip Hobshaun, whose opinion it was that "Irvine Welsh will be here today and gone tomorrow." Somewhere between the literary conservatives who reviled him and the ravers who revered him were those who, like Jenny Turner, worried, or at least wondered, whether he "may have written himself into a rut" (Curtis, 1996).

For his part, Welsh, while understandably appreciative of all that it had done for him, likened *Trainspotting* to "a bad curry after a few pints of lager. It keeps coming back" when he was interested in moving on (Smith, 1996). Moving ahead meant writing more and talking less, about himself and his work. And it meant, in writing the screenplays for *The Acid House Trilogy*, remaining more faithful to his sources than the writer John Hodge, director Danny Boyle and producer Andrew MacDonald had been with *Trainspotting*. *The Acid House Trilogy* would be just what the ads proclaimed, "The pure and uncut Irvine Welsh." Welsh had tried his hand at writing a screenplay a few years earlier for the Scottish Shorts series begun in 1993, only to have his work rejected (rightly so, Welsh felt). *The Acid House Trilogy* succeeds almost too well in transforming page to screen; there are no concessions made to the mass audience and none of the film *Trainspotting*'s airbrushing and user-friendliness—and none of its commercial success either. The first of its three parts, *Granton Star Cause*, was aired in the UK on Channel 4 at 11 P.M. on 4 August 1997 amidst calls, mainly from religious groups outraged by Welsh's depiction of God as an old, meanspirited drunk, that it be banned outright or at least censored.

Acid House may not have pleased religious conservatives or the mass audience but it did please Welsh, who was happy "to downsize in a way, become more cult-y again" (Bresnark, 1999).

Welsh went on to have a very active and visible year. In addition to the airing of *Granton Star Cause*, Welsh appeared (with Kate Moss) in rocker Bobby Gillespie's new music video, recorded the single "I Sentence You To a Life of Dance," and published a regular column in the New Lad magazine *Loaded*. He went on a book tour of the United States, with fellow hot Scots Kelman and McLean (with the US press taking a certain delight, as the UK press had a few years earlier, in Welsh's capacity for drink, drugs and boorish behavior). Back in the UK, Jonathan Cape/Secker & Warburg released the 920-page *Irvine Welsh Omnibus*, which reprints in one volume the full texts of *Trainspotting, The Acid House*, and *Marabou Stork Nightmares*. In July, Welsh's *Headstate*, which had premiered at the Edinburgh Fringe the year before, was featured at the Greenwich and Docklands International Festival. Growing out of discussions some years earlier with Boilerhouse director Paul Pinsof, *Headstate* was intended as a pre-club event and "the antithesis of the ugly, smug, bland *Four Weddings and a Funeral* style which," Welsh contends, "hilariously passes for 'art' today" (Welsh, "Drugs and the Theatre, Darlings").

All the attention only seemed to rekindle questions about Welsh's durability and importance — and the wisdom of certain of his aesthetic choices. To some, the subjects, even the titles, of his two major works of 1998 indicated that a career that had begun so brilliantly with Welsh's unflinching exposé of junky life had reached the dead-end of brutality and sensationalism for their own sake. Welsh's first stage play, the "calculatingly nasty" *You'll Have Had Your Hole*, which one reviewer said made *Trainspotting* look like *Teletubbies*, premiered at the Yorkshire Playhouse in Leeds in August to withering reviews before moving on to London in somewhat revised form, though with its Jacobean revenge plot, torture, and anal rape still intact and the British Council cancelling its plans to stage the play abroad. Welsh, always one to try something new, tried his hand at playwriting only because Ian Brown, the director of two highly regarded productions of *Trainspotting*, suggested that he should. Once he had both time and inclination, Welsh did and was in general far more pleased with the communal production experience than critics were with the play itself. He was also surprised at how easy playwriting was — and how, as a result, potentially damaging to the novelist. If the team aspect helped persuade Welsh to undertake other collaborative endeavors (guest editor of *The Big Issue* and co-author of the screenplay for the 1999 television drama *Dockers*), the damage playwriting did to the novelist seemed to some fully evident in *Filth*, Welsh's then longest and, for many, least successful novel (critically, not commercially; *Filth* too was a bestseller in Britain).

The fact that *Filth* appeared just as the British literary establishment was throwing its full weight behind a massive American import made Welsh's situation appear even worse. "As for Irvine Welsh, well, it always looked more like word-processing than writing, but surely now the game's up for the foul-mouthed chancer? Compare his most recent novel, the dire, remorselessly vulgar *Filth* to, say, Don DeLillo's *Underworld* and it is clear that while American literature's concerns are politics, history, adultery, money and war, Welsh's go no further than a tapeworm and the c-word" (Maconie, 1998). While some saw Welsh at a crossroads and gave him to year's end to see whether "he will be viewed as the future of British literature or as yesterday's man" (Smith, A., 1998), others believed the matter (once again) already decided: "Irvine Welsh — he's so mid-nineties. For that brief instant a while back, Welsh was simply essential: you had to read his books, see the adaptations. . . . He is now simply a set text for a particular generational/cultural syllabus, with all the freshness and threat that implies" ("Designed to Shock," 1998). Harry Gibson's adaptation of *Filth*—a two-hour monologue performed by Tam Dean Burn that premiered in Glasgow in March 2000—may, as one reviewer noted, have "helped restore Welsh's bruised reputation," but other life signs were less encouraging. In mid-1995, Welsh and Ian Banks dominated the Scottish bestseller list (three titles each). Five years later, Ian Rankin, author of Edinburgh mysteries, occupied six of the top ten slots and J. K. Rowling's Harry Potter books another three. In 1995 BBC2 aired a show on Welsh. In 2000, the leader for an article in the London *Times* Television and Radio section ran, "From illegal raves to superclubs, the history of club culture is dissected by old-timers Boy George and Irvine Welsh in *The Chemical Generation*." Announcements of Welsh's having become *passé* seem decidedly premature. In addition to stories in two recent collections (Nick Hornby's *Speaking with the Angel* and Richard Thomas's *Vox 'n' Roll*), Welsh published his longest and most ambitious novel, *Glue*, in May 2001, with the long-awaited *Trainspotting* sequel, *Porno*, scheduled for release in May 2002. He is also working on a film adaptation of another *Acid House* story, "A Smart Cunt," writing the lyrics for the Bay City Rollers' comeback album, and collaborating with Vic Godard on a musical. However, announcements of Welsh's literary demise may not only be premature; they may be beside the point. Welsh, remember, has never narrowly defined himself as "a writer." Having "stumbled" into writing, he might just stumble out, if he ever feels he has nothing more to say, having, already, in just eight years—indeed, with just one book—vastly expanded the contemporary writer's, especially the contemporary Scottish writer's, role, influence, and audience and brought about one of the most dramatic changes in "British" literary history.

CONTEXT AND INFLUENCES

Irvine Welsh is not a "writer" in the sense that, say, Martin Amis is. Rather, Welsh is a cultural phenomenon of sociological as well as aesthetic significance. Of course, every literary work is more a cultural product than an autonomous aesthetic object, but few works are quite as rewarding when read from a cultural studies approach as *Trainspotting*, a multiform work whose "incendiary debut" leads us to examine not only the text itself but its multiple antecedents and post-publication effects: historical, political, literary, economic, and cultural.

One of these is the political situation in Scotland since 1979. That was the year that Margaret Thatcher began her eleven year reign as Tory Prime Minister and the year that the referendum on Scottish self-rule failed. That failure had a profound effect on Scots over the next two decades, in part because the failure was at once abject and ambiguous. (Although a majority of voters said yes, the referendum failed because of a clause, added late, which stipulated that in order for the measure to pass, it had to be approved by forty percent of the *total* electorate.) Even as the Tories suffered continued setbacks in Scotland in the 1980s, Thatcher's economic policies continued to affect Scotland adversely, further marginalizing it and making the strong tradition of Scottish socialism seem increasingly irrelevant. The worsening situation resulted in the meeting of the Scottish National Convention in 1989 and the riots in response to the Thatcher government's regressive restructuring of the poll tax the following year. Seven years (and several Irvine Welsh books) later, the Tories were out and Labour under Tony Blair was in, paving the way for passage of a new referendum on devolution and the opening of the Scottish parliament in 2000, its first in nearly three centuries.

The effect of Tory economic and social policies on Scottish life, and therefore indirectly on *Trainspotting*, was not all a matter of negative reaction. The party that had made such effective use of media and advertising in coming to power in 1979 ushered in both a winner-take-all mentality that deeply divided the nation geographically and economically and a more dynamic, hyper-capitalist economy which would greatly change the ways in which advertisers, publishers, broadcasters and others did business by the time *Trainspotting* appeared. Thatcher's policies of denationalization, decentralization, and competitive markets had already helped reform the radio, television and film fields that were instrumental in helping redefine Scottish identity. The changes occurring in Scottish theater were no less dramatic. The end of theater censorship in 1968 ushered in an age of contemporary, often politically charged plays staged in non-traditional venues. Randall Stevenson may stretch things a bit in positing a connection between the "transgressive energies" of drama's "ancient origins" and the new "post-Presbyterian" fiction of Welsh and others, but he is certainly correct in believing that it is only since the 1970s that there has been "much Scottish theatre to celebrate" and that there is a link between this theatrical renaissance, which included Simon Donald's well-received play, *The Life of Stuff* (1992), about "drugs, crime, and urban desolation" (Petrie, 2000, p. 197), and the slightly later renaissance of Scottish fiction.

Both have played their part in forging a new sense of Scottish identity, for "in the absence of an elected political authority the task of representing the nation has been repeatedly devolved" to its writers (Whyte, 1998, p. 284). And this is especially the case at a time when the devolution issue was most on people's minds and their sense of Scottish impotence and marginalization most acute. It is significant that the apparent failure of (Scottish) national socialism during the Thatcher years coincided with writers', especially fiction writers', search for and utilization of innovative narrative strategies, starting with Alisdair Gray's *Lanark*. Rejecting "the prevailing sentimental, romantic or 'realistic' paradigms," these writers present a Scotland that is fragmented, alienated, urban, in crisis, and decidedly non-essentialist — so much so that "the cultural fragmentation which earlier writers deplored was recast throughout the 1990s as vital, invigorating diversity" (McIlvanney, 2000). Out with the kitsch of kilts and shortbread, and in with *Lanark* and Kelman's *How Late It Was, How Late*.

Kelman is especially important to a full and accurate understanding of *Trainspotting*. He was the first Scot to win Britain's most prestigious (some would say most hyped) literary prize, the Booker, in its (then) twenty five years of existence. Although Kelman won in 1994, one year after *Trainspotting* had been published (and nominated), his award and the attention it brought to Scottish fiction came at the very time that interest in Welsh and his first novel were just accelerating. Even as it built upon what Gavin Wallace has called the Scottish novel's "spectacular tradition of despair," *How Late It Was* offered a new and more authentic (though nonetheless aesthetically crafted) language for articulating this despair, one that did not so much provide a model to follow as a focus on "voice as the basis of art" for the new generation of Scottish writers (McLean, 1998, xii). Equally important, Kelman's Booker validated what these new writers already knew, that, as Whyte and Galloway put it, " 'Scottish literature' as a cozy study of the past is not enough: we must support the vital and volatile brat that is literature in the making." The support predated 1994 in the form of little magazines, publishers such as Clocktower, Canongate, and Polygon, but would dramatically increase afterwards. However, Kelman's success had one other notable effect. Even as it contributed to Scottish writers' sense of community and purpose, it also created a sense of and need for difference. Kelman's Glasgow, despite having been designated "European City of Culture," seemed to have a literary lock on urban blight and doomed vernacular. Welsh's "Edinburgh dirty realism" provides an alternative style and vision, one that derives from the culture of disaffected youth rather than working class solidarity that Welsh maintains was, as a viable political position, destroyed in the eighties.

Another reason for the sudden interest in Scottish writers is the more general interest on the part of British readers, publishers and reviewers in "New Commonwealth" authors such as Welsh and Roddy Doyle which Welsh attributed to "colonial guilt" and to the consumer culture's insatiable craving for something new and to "colonial guilt." Odd as it may at first seem, post-colonialism provides an appropriate context for understanding part of *Trainspotting*'s effect and appeal both in terms of its subversion of standard English as well as the cultural imperialism it implies and the hybrid existences of characters living, in Homi K. Bhabha's terms, border lives that require a "new art of the present" and a proliferation of "englishes." For the new Scottish writers, this entails, as Robin Robertson puts it, a "complete rejection of London as cultural and linguistic centre" (Cowley, 1997), and a similar rejection of a similarly monolithic Scottish cultural centre.

Trainspotting's literary context and antecedents (analogues as well as actual influences) extend still further. They extend back at least as far as the Angry Young Men of the 1950s and Edinburgh's chief beat writer and heroin addict in exile, Alexander Trocchi. Chronologically closer to Welsh and those reviewing *Trainspotting* are the Brat Pack writers of "blank fiction" — Jay McInerney, Tama Janowitz, and Bret Easton Ellis — whose studied superficiality, black comedy, and cast of disaffected yuppie addicts prepared the way for the films of Quentin Tarantino. Closer still are the aging, directionless young men of New Lad-lite writer Nick Hornby and the "calculated nastiness" and "postapocalyptic realism" of Will Self and

Iain Banks ("Bard of Scottish depravity, madness, and mayhem"), and the Turner Prize-winning Brit Art of Damien Hirst and others all played out against the smarmy background made up of equal parts Princess Di, *Four Weddings and a Funeral*, and Louis de Bernieres' *Captain Corelli's Mandolin*, "a captivating love story set on the Ionian island of Cephalonia during he second World War," which sold nearly a million copies from 1994 to 1998. No account of Welsh's antecedents would be complete that did not mention popular music, from punk to techno. (Tartan techno was especially strong in the early 90s.) For Welsh, music-centered youth culture, more than literary pedigree, provides the acceptable alternative to Thatcher's competitive individualism, John Major's "laughable 'classless society,'" and "the touchy-feely Blair era of superficial smarm" that Welsh scorns ("It's Generational and Geographical," 1994; Macdonald, 1996).

2

The Novel

LANGUAGE

Odd as it may seem for a novel about drugs as a social issue about which its author felt deeply concerned and personally involved—an author with no formal training in writing or in literature at a time when British fiction was dominated by writers who were either university trained and sometimes university based or part of the London literary establishment, a writer whose roots were in popular youth culture (from punk to rave) and the Scottish urban underclass—*Trainspotting* proved not just critically and commercially successful but successful in large part because of, not in spite of, its language. Indeed, it was the "linguistic resourcefulness" of a writer whose aesthetic was decidedly anti-art and whose stance was no less anti-art establishment that drew special praise and that both requires and repays close attention. As Charles Spencer pointed out, "It's the power of Welsh's language that makes the nightmare so vivid." The most salient feature of Welsh's powerful language is fully evident in the novel's opening words: "The sweat wis lashing oafay Sick Boy." Here is a world that offers no introduction and no apology, a world that simply presents itself on its own terms, in its own words and with its own frame(s) of cultural reference. The section title, "The Skag Boys, Jean-Claude Van Damme, and Mother Superior," draws on three intersecting referential systems: drugs, film (of the martial arts, action movie kind), and local (Mother Superior being the dealer Johnny Swan's nickname). And it draws on its own linguistic system as well which connects *Train-spotting* to a specific locality (Leith) and to an aspect of the Scottish literary tradition that goes back to Robert Burns and that more especially recalls Edwin Muir's analysis of "the predicament of the Scottish writer." This is his ("Scottish writer" being until recently an almost exclusively male designation) being "afflicted by the in-eradicable psychological damage of a divided linguistic inheritance" and therefore "forced to feel in one language and think [and write] in another" (Craig, 1999, 11).

Welsh's handling of dialect, so often the marker of quaintness and/or social inferiority, is anything but artless and is, interestingly enough, reminiscent of another "vernacular spectacular" reviled in its day for the coarseness of its language and its deleterious effect on the nation's youth: Mark Twain's *Adventures of Huckleberry Finn*. Comparison of Welsh's novel, which he began writing in standard English, with sections published earlier in *Past Tense* and elsewhere indicate that Welsh, perhaps responding to editors' suggestions, kept fine-tuning the novel's dialect, sometimes making it heavier, some-times lighter. (According to Andy Beckett, Welsh also tinkered with the tone, lightening an original that had been "morbid, almost gothic, and full of rage" [25 July 1998]). This "strangled Scottish vernacular," which, as Ian Bell has noted, is especially "strong on the rhythms of speech, the sub-poetry of slang and obscenity" (15 August 1993), affects the reader in multiple ways as it articulates, represents and even embodies its characters' lives. One of the ways it does this is by creating "a haze of language" which blurs individual identities, making the characters less distinct than their general environment and the pervasive subcultural mindset. Another way is by working in the opposite direction, creating differences within the apparent sameness of Leith-speak that serve to individualize the novel's numerous speakers. As Nicholas Williams has explained, "Welsh skillfully distinguishes between the many first-person narrators in his novel by giving them voices composed in varying degrees of Scots and English content, as well as creating verbal tics (like Spud's terminal 'ken?' [and 'like say'] or Sick Boy's constant reference to himself in the third person) which both reveal character and serve as helpful signposts in a potentially confusing narrative collage" (1999, 228–229).

Although Welsh's use of demotic Scots is indebted to Kelman and was generally reviewed as such, it is also apparent, as Christopher Whyte observes, that more attentive, culturally attuned readers will discern in the "written stylization of 'uneducated' speech" that Welsh devised less an imitation of Kelman's working-class Glaswegian than a challenge to it. Welsh's is a Leith-based alternative that not only allows and empowers its previously un(der)represented and therefore effectively silenced characters to speak. It also proves more demanding of, and makes fewer concessions to, Standard English speakers, in part by confronting them with greater dialectical variation and fewer opportunities to escape into the refuge that Standard English affords. As John Skinner has noted, "Welsh's metropolitan Scots is actually far more impressive in range and variety than the more homogeneous Glaswegian demotic forged by Kelman" (1999, 218). And not just more varied; less sanitized too. "The problem I have with Kelman," Welsh has said, "is that he seems ideologically to censor his characters. They are always non-sexist and non-racist. But I don't feel you can put these parameters on the characters you've created. If they seem xenophobic or bigoted you have to let them speak that way" (Smith, C. L., 1995).

Another important point to keep in mind about dialect in *Trainspotting* is that while it "is not in any true or historical sense Scots," as Allan Massie has pointed out, neither is it nothing more than "spelling English words as the characters' pronunciation of them sounds to the author's ear." Rather, dialect in the novel is a hybrid linguistic form that marginalizes the standard English on which it depends. It should therefore be understood in relation to the point Robert Crawford makes in *Devolving English Literature* (1992), namely "how an un-English identity may be preserved or developed within 'English literature'" (6). The use of dialect to marginalize standard English is underscored in two ways in Welsh's novel. One involves what the novel excludes: the glossary that a friend advised and Welsh refused to add. "The last thing I want is all these fuckers up in Charlotte Square putting on the vernacular as a stage managed thing. It's nothing to do with them" (Farquarson, 1993), although a glossary was appended to the US edition. The other way this marginalization is underscored involves what the novel includes: the narrating of four of its forty three unnumbered sections in standard English: "Growing up in Public," "Grieving and Mourning in Port Sunshine," "The First Shag in Ages" (all three in the third person), and "Bad Blood" (narrated in the first). Welsh's use of dialect makes standard English appear abnormal and freakish. It also "resists the transparency of much novelistic discourse to draw attention to itself as writing from the body" (Williams, 1999, 227), including the body politic. Welsh's linguistic assertion of Scottish identity is in fact an assertion more particularly of a Scottish subcultural identity within a *mise-en-abime* of identity politics: youth within working class Leith within cultured Edinburgh within Scotland within a Britain centered in London and based in the English language. Welsh's use of dialect in *Trainspotting* is, however, still more complex, in effect if not necessarily by intention. For as Cairns Craig suggests, "like the empty shell of Leith Central Station" that looms so ominously near novel's end, "it gestures to the lost community which dialect had represented in the Scottish tradition and which has now been corrupted into fearful individualism" (1999, 97). As such, dialect functions in much the same way that the singing of the Irish ballad, "The Boys of the Old Brigade," does for Begbie and the others on New Year's eve: "Stevie worried about the singing. It had a desperate edge to it. It was as if by singing loudly enough, they would weld themselves together into a powerful brotherhood" (46).

Craig's warning concerning gutted community and fearful individualism aside for the moment, the novel's dialect is one of several features that together make up Welsh's "dazzlingly self-assured" style — "the voice of punk grown up, grown wise and grown eloquent" (Hughes-Hallett, 1993). Another is the narrative's "verbal energy" and "unstoppable vitality." Equally important is the "rawness" of the novel's "gritty style" which connects *Trainspotting* to the traditions of literary realism and naturalism so evident in the precision with which Welsh transcribes his characters' speech, describes their environment, renders their daily lives, and graphically details activities such as cooking a hit of heroin, shooting up, and withdrawal. Even so, *Trainspotting* resists being classified as realism or naturalism. Alan Freeman has even wondered whether it is Welsh's "pulling apart the conventions of realism" that may be "the key to the power of his utterance, his world of unrealities eluding a final, stable reality on which to alight" (1996, 257). If the *Scotsman* is right to liken Welsh's writing to "graffiti whose illicit action and fierce street colours turn fully into art" ("It's"), then one way to understand what Welsh has accomplished is to recall his main character, Mark Renton, sitting in a filthy toilet, catching "a huge, filthy bluebottle, a big, furry currant ay a bastard" and smearing it against the wall to form the letters of his favorite football team, Hibs (Hibernians): "The vile bluebottle, which caused me a great deal of distress, has been transformed intae a work of art which gives me much pleasure tae look at" (25). But perhaps the better analogy is to the job Mark dredges up from "his portfolio of bogus employment identities": "curator at the museums section of the District Council's Recreation Department." "Ah rake around in people's rubbish for things that've been discarded, and present them as authentic historical artefacts ay working people's everyday lives. The ah make sure that they dinnae fall apart when they're oan exhibition" (146–147).

Trainspotting's realism is apparent but made to coexist with and to some degree is undermined by other stylistic features, including the novel's pervasive humor, which manifests itself in several forms. The humor is there in section titles such as "Inter Shitty" (the British Rail train designation "InterCity" rendered with a Sean Connery accent). Some of the comedy is situational and plays off seemingly innocuous, certainly middle class section titles. In "Traditional Sunday Breakfast," for example, a badly hungover and confused David Mitchell awakes in a strange bed which he quickly realizes is (1) awash with his own urine, vomit and excrement and (2) in the parental home of a girl he'd like to shag, Gail Hudson. In the kitchen, Mrs. Hudson invites David to breakfast and insists that she will wash the sheets he has bundled up and wants to take with him to clean. A tug-of-war ensues, reaching a more-than-Chaplinesque, cream-pie-in-the-face conclusion: "The sheets flew open and a pungent shower of skittery shite, thin alcohol sick, and vile pish splashed out across the floor," leaving Mrs. Hudson "heaving into the sink" and "Brown flecks of runny shite stain[ing] Mr Hudson's glasses, face and white shirt," as well as his food and daughter (94).

Welsh's humor is not only often intensely physical and scatalogical but increasingly edgy and grim. The edginess is especially apparent in the sexist joke Sick Boy plays on Kelly in "The Elusive Mr Hunt," when he calls the bar where she works and asks if Mark Hunt is there. Her shouting out "Mark Hunt," which given her accent comes out sounding like "my" or "more cunt," leaves her embarrassed and the bar's largely male patrons more than amused: "It's not funny laughter," Renton realizes. "This is lynch mob laughter" (279). The humor of "A Leg Over" proves similarly troubling. The title refers to having sex but the section itself deals with an addict who, although he continues to fantasize about sex (in Thailand), won't be getting one of his legs over because it has just been amputated. Having had his veins collapse after years of injecting, he began shooting into his arteries, including the one in his leg that subsequently became infected. Thus downward the course of causality and black comedy in the world according to Welsh.

If, as Iggy Pop sings at the Barrowlands concert that two of the novel's characters attend, nicely adapting his lyrics to his audience, "Scotland takes drugs in psychic defense," then *Trainspotting* uses black humor for much the same reason. This is what Nina realizes at the wake for her Uncle Andy: "that laughter was about more than humour. This was about reducing tension, solidarity in the face of the grim reaper" (33). However, Nina's realization is itself mocked and the solidarity debunked rather than confirmed. Nina sees the corpse sweating and cries out that Uncle Andy is alive; the others arrive, including the doctor who discovers that the electric blanket that was placed over the body had been accidentally left on. "Bad Blood" (another section title) figuratively refers to the animosity between its two main characters (an animosity worthy of Shakespeare or Poe) but literally refers to the fact that both characters are HIV-positive, the one in fact indirectly responsible for the other's becoming infected and therefore for the little joke the latter will play on the former to its fatal conclusion. Here and elsewhere,

Trainspotting's grim comedy differs from the black humor fiction of the 1960s in which seemingly terminal despair is offset by the authors' essentially melioristic sensibility. Welsh's fiction, although not without a heavy dose of social conscience, even outrage, strikes a more despairing note, not because *Trainspotting* is "unremittingly bleak" but instead because it is so "sophisticatedly nihilistic" (Self, 1996).

Considered "overweening" and "designed to depress the liberal reader" by some, "liberating" by others, this "energetic negativity, that is part of the book's *fin de siecle* appeal" (Crawford, 2000, 334), is as much in the details as it is either dramatized in the larger narrative situations or highlighted in section titles. It is there, for example, in "Bad Blood," in the offhand mention of Edinburgh's Museum of Childhood in a mini-narrative in which one character will anesthetize and then stage the torture and murder of a young boy so that he can show the photographs to the supposedly "dead" boy's actually dying father in order to avenge past wrongs. And it is there in "A Leg Over," in the addict-amputee's "reaching for a decaffeinated Diet Coke." The humor here, in context anyway, is both subtle and of a decidedly postmodern kind. The Museum of Childhood and decaffeinated Diet Coke are signs of the hyper-real as well as of the late-capitalist Britain that has little knowledge of and (until *Trainspotting*) even less interest in the all too real world that Welsh depicts. It is easy either to overvalue or underestimate Welsh's brand of humor, either taking momentary pleasure in the postmodern cool of his sophisticatedly nihilistic style or dismissing it because Welsh's humor lacks sufficient (or overt) satirical bite. Thus, John Gross's complaint: lacking Jonathan Swift's "excremental vision," Welsh offers up the "excrement without the vision" and "smart tough-guy complacency in lieu heartfelt anguish." Such a position requires that we hold Welsh to precisely the kind of timeless, universal standard that his fiction, and that of many con-

temporary Scottish writers, has challenged. And it is to misunder-
stand the part humor plays in making *Trainspotting* what it is,
arguably the most oddly or acutely angled of those characteristically
Scottish "elegies to the dispossessed."

Like humor, fantasy plays an important part in *Trainspotting*.
Welsh's descriptions of shooting up and coming clean may border
on the clinical in their realism, but the look on Sick Boy's face—
"ugly, leering and reptilian, before he slams the cocktail towards
her [Alison's] brain"—is not, any more than his look a moment
later after his own hit, his eyes "now innocent and full ay wonder,
his expression like a bairn thit's come through oan Christmas morning tae a pile ay gift-wrapped presents stacked under the tree" (9).
At times the fantasy seeks to represent accurately a character's state
of mind—for example, Mark's just after shooting up, feeling "Ma
dry, cracking bones . . . soothed and liquefied by ma beautiful heroine's tender caresses" (11) or, *Trainspotting*'s longest and best
known instance, Mark's hallucinating during withdrawal, especially
when he sees Lesley's dead baby, Wee Dawn, climbing down from
the ceiling. At other times the fantasy creates a rather different visual
effect, closer to cartoon than to dream. The cartoon-like effect is
especially noticeable in sex scenes: as Dianne "[rides] herself into a
climax," Renton lies "there like a dildo on a large skateboard" until
he too climaxes, "his cock spurt[ing] like a water pistol in the hands
of a persistently mischievous child. Abstinence had made the sperm
count go through the roof" (141). The scene involving Spud and
Laura McEwan, "whose cruelty and ruthlessness was [sic] part of
her attraction," and involving bondage and the promise of anal
intercourse, reads like an R. Crumb comic strip or X-rated *Fritz the
Cat* animated film of Chaplinesque sexual misadventures and pain-
ful as well as painfully funny pratfalls. Welsh's metaphors often
transform, or transmogrify, the merely commonplace into intensely
visual and physical cartoon images. There is Tommy who looks "as

if he's an incomplete jigsaw puzzle," Jocky whose "pus is shaped like an egg on its side" and who "spat out his syllables Kalashnikov style," "the lassie with eyes like Marty Feldman and the hair like pubes," the old drunk whose blood vessels have ruptured under his skin "leaving it resembling the undercooked square sausages served in the local cafes," and the bus station concourse which Welsh likens to "a Social Security office turned inside out and doused with oil."

The merely fantastic and cartoonish often topple over into the realm of the truly grotesque that is reminiscent of Poe of H. P. Lovecraft (a writer whom Renton mentions at one point). "It was a sound, rather than a voice," a narrator says of a patient dying of AIDS-related complications. "It seemed to come from an unspecific part of his decaying body rather than his mouth" (257). Elsewhere, the effect is more Hogathtian as Welsh sketches a tableau of Edinburgh lowlife: "What huv ah goat here? Billy's fuckin nosey, reactionary bastard's outrage. Sharon lookin at us like ah've goat two heids. Ma, drunk and sluttish, Sick Boy . . . the cunt. Spud in the jail. Matty in the hospital, and nae cunt's been to see him, nae cunt even talks aboot him, it's like he never existed. Begbie . . . fuck sakes, glowing, while [the pregnant] June looks like a pile ay crumpled bones in that hideous shell-suit, an unflattering garment at the best ay times, but highlighting her jagged shapelessness" (176–177). Individually, the characters appear equally grotesque: Second Prize's face "resembled that of an ugly bird whose eggs are under threat from a stalking predator," Sick Boy has "bulging chameleon [elsewhere: frog] eye's," Begbie looks particularly "seedy and menacing done up in a suit . . . indian ink spilling oot from under cuffs and collar onto neck and hands" as if his "tattoos move intae the light, resentful at being covered up" (77) or Nelly looking similarly "incongruous in a suit, with a tattooed snake coiling up his neck and a palm-treed desert island with the sea lapping up drilled onto his forehead" (290).

Not in every one of its parts but certainly in its overall effect, *Trainspotting* belongs to the literary genre Mikhail Bakhtin termed grotesque realism. Bakhtin coined the term to describe the twin narratives, *Gargantua* and *Pantagruel*, by the Sixteenth Century French doctor and writer, Francois Rabelais, who was every bit as controversial, iconoclastic and cartoonishly crude in his depictions of the body and bodily functions in his day as Welsh is in ours. For Bakhtin, exaggeration and degradation are grotesque realism's defining characteristics. In *Trainspotting*, exaggeration, which Bakhtin associates with "fertility, growth . . . abundance," appears only in its negative aspect. Degradation, on the other hand, in Welsh closely follows the Bakhtinian model in that it acts as a positive subversive force which "transfers to the material level . . . all that is high, spiritual, ideal, abstract" (*Rabelais*, 19). Moreover, grotesque realism is a key element of carnivalization, which Bakhtin defines as "the transposition of carnival into the language of literature." Multi-style and multi-form, carnival literature involves the suspension of the hierarchical structure of monologic authority and the material creation of decrowning doubles, "joyful relativity" and "free and familiar contact between people." However, as Bakhtin realized and as a carnivalized text such as *Trainspotting* clearly implies, carnival depends upon the existence of an authentic folk culture and community without which carnival must itself degenerate, coming to exist solely in its negative aspect, which is to say (to use Michael Andre Bernstein's apt phrase) when the carnival turns bitter and Nietzschean resentment replaces carnival regeneration. At this point, there is no affirmation of the person as a vital part of an organic community, only the triumph of the bourgeois self and the marketplace ethos of competitive individualism (against which Welsh's later fiction posits the positive communal aspect of rave culture.)

Intuitively following the Bakhtinian model, Welsh calls attention to the material body, emphasizing in Rabelaisian fashion its sheer physicality as distinct from the abstractions of politicians, social scientists, liberal humanists, and, one might add, postmodern theorists. As we have already seen, Welsh's preoccupation with the physical body is often funny, but it is just as often discomforting, as in his description of the "the bloated sow," "a gross bitch with a broken leg" Renton finds in Mike Forrester's flat: the "repulsive swell of white flesh between the dirty plaster and her peach coloured shorts," her "oversized Guinness pot," "her white flab," "her greasy, peroxide locks" with "an inch of insipid grey-brown at their roots" and her "horrendous and embarrassing donkey-like laugh" (19), with the presence of "beefy-faced but thin-bodied" Forrester intensifying rather than mitigating the unpleasantness. Less graphically but more perversely for the reader who fails to appreciate *Trainspotting* as a work of grotesque realism is Welsh's Rabelaisian preoccupation with human orifices — mouths, anuses and vaginas, as well as needle holes — and with body fluids and biological processes (from eating, drinking and copulating to urinating, defecating, menstruating, and vomiting). Often food, sex, and waste are brought into close proximity: in the "Traditional Sunday Breakfast" section and much later in "Eating Out" in which Kelly, a waitress, avenges herself on a party of drunk and abusive "middle to upper-middle-class English" men by adding her urine, excrement, and menstrual blood, plus a little rat poison, to their food and drink. In perhaps the novel's (certainly the film's) most memorable scene, Mark successfully trolls the dark waters of a clogged public toilet for the two opium suppositories he has just unthinkingly defecated into the bowl, then contemplates swallowing them both before rejecting the idea because the waxy coating would make it difficult to keep them down.

Far from being a sign that Welsh is either depraved or a case of arrested development, this emphasis on bodily realities serves much the same purpose they do in Rabelais or, closer to home, in certain of the works of Hugh MacDiarmid: weapons in a war "against gentility and bourgeois evasiveness" (Critty, 2001). Welsh's grotesquerie, like MacDiarmid's, implies the damage done the Scottish body: physical, psychological, political, and economic. This is the damage symbolized (but not merely "symbolized") by the HIV which not only penetrates the body but inscribes itself on the body as well, the way the crime is inscribed on the guilty body in Franz Kafka's "In the Penal Colony." The grim grotesquerie also manifests itself typographically on the novel's pages, although nowhere as extensively and interestingly as in *Marabou Stork Nightmares*, with its multiple typefaces and ascending and descending narratives, or *Filth*, with the vermicular-shaped narrative of its voluble and voracious tapeworm literally overriding (or overwriting) that of the novel's protagonist and tapeworm's host, DS Bruce Robertson. In *Trainspotting*, the visual effect may be less noticeable but it is no less important in creating a sense of the text as a physical object: the four numbered parts of "Speedy Recruitment," the "exchange of cards" in "Bang to Rites," the "typical exchange" between Mark and a psychiatrist in "Searching for the Inner Man," the use of page-layout to indicate changes in Mark's levels of consciousness during withdrawal in "House Arrest" (something of a practice run for *Marabou Stork Nightmares*, especially the Molly Bloom-on-speed monologue of the vampiric ghost of Wee Dawn), the italicized "junk dilemmas" and the italicized passages throughout which signal deeper levels of the characters' interior monologues.

Another way *Trainspotting* calls attention to the physicality of its language is through various forms of mimicry used to materialize and debunk utterances that pretend to be monologic, authoritative and universal (including "the royal we" and "sounding posh"). The mimicry is especially noticeable and effective in "Bang to Rites." Mark's older brother, Billy, who had recently reenlisted in the British army, is killed in an ambush while on patrol in Northern

Ireland. He is mourned by his family, especially by the paternal, Protestant side whose sectarian Orange bigotry helped fuel Billy's violent sense of patriotic duty, and eulogized by "some ruling class cunt, a junior minister or something, say[ing] in his Oxbridge voice how Billy wis a brave young man" (211). In Mark's bitterly resentful monologue, however, Billy appears not as the brave son and soldier but as "a spare prick in a uniform" getting "a posthumous fifteen minutes ay fame." "He wis exactly the kind ay cunt they'd huv branded as a cowardly thug if he wis in civvy street rather than on Her Majesty's Service" (210–11). As the minister praises someone he never knew in one-size-fits-all cliches and a "wimpy cunt ay an officer" drapes a Union Jack over the coffin, Mark internally unveils and resurrects an incontinent and abusive decrowning double who "died as he lived: completely fuckin scoobied."

The mimicry is equally apparent in "Searching for the Inner Man," where Mark represents the three therapeutic practices and styles with which he has been (unsuccessfully) treated, or rather subjected: psychiatry (Dr. Forbes), clinical psychology (Molly Greaves), and drugs counseling (Tom Curzon). Mark's recontextualized repetition of the analyst's words in the deprecatingly parodic "typical exchange" with the psychiatrist—Forbes's reductive Freudian ideas and his portentous, very unPinterlike pauses and "ah's" included—creates much the same effect Jorge Luis Borges writes about in his well-known metafiction, "Pierre Menard, Author of *Don Quixote*." Against these therapeutic models, Mark posits the folk wisdom, as it were, of his former girlfriend, Hazel. Although not entirely free of the junk of theory and its jargon ("Hazel understands ego needs. She's a windae dresser in a department store, but describes hersel as a 'consumer display artist' or something like that"), she assesses Mark's condition this way: "you just want tae fuck up on drugs so that everyone'll think how deep and fucking complex you are. It's pathetic, and fucking boring" (186–187). It is

Hazel's view, not the views of any of the "therapy/counseling shites," that leads Mark to his now famous, post-punk declaration of independence from Choosing Life. And, oddly enough, it is Mark who ends up playing the part — and rather sincerely too, if briefly — for his dead brother's pregnant, formerly abused girlfriend, Sharon — this just after shagging her doggy style on the bathroom floor in his parents' home and just before sending her on her way so that he can cook up another hit for himself. *Trainspotting* underscores the falsity, inauthenticity, and perniciousness of all forms of "the reminiscing game" — eulogies, patriotic songs such as "James Connolly," etc. — while giving high marks to those who resist playing the game (the minister at Venters' funeral who "to his credit . . . didn't bullshit") or who, deciding that discretion is the better part of self-preservation, play it self-consciously: Mark trying to sound like James Cagney and "failing pathetically" or at Billy's funeral, "stick[ing] tae the cliches" rather than saying what is on his mind, without, however, "compromising too much tae the sickening hypocrisy, perversely peddled as decency" (214).

STRUCTURE

Trainspotting is just as interesting and complex in matters of structure as it is in matters of style. Not that you would know that from the many reviews that sought to explain, and therefore contain, that structure pejoratively, saying that *Trainspotting* was "less a novel than a set of loosely linked improvisations," a "series of monologues strung together by the thinnest pretext," a merely "anecdotal narrative" or "collage" that evidenced no more artistry than an old drunk's pub tales. Yet while many found the structure "ramshackle," others detected an effective if not necessarily conscious "layering" of incidents and voices from which "a real picture of Edinburgh lowlife emerges" (Howard, 1996). Will Self "saw" the novel meta-phorically, as "a torch of awareness" passed from one character (and interior monologue) to the next. Welsh imagined the novel differ-ently, as "a bunch of voices shouting to be heard"; "you're inside their heads rather than [as in the film version] watching them on the screen" (McGavin, 1996). Although the structure of *Trainspot-ting* resembles *Headstate*'s "linked sketches," its effect is more pro-nounced, the fracturing more intense, so that overall the narrative "feels like an exercise in futility," producing out of the squalor of Edinburgh's post-industrial fringe "the hell of a narrative without end, without purpose" about characters who "exist in an internal present" (Craig, 1996, 131; Bell, 15 August 1993; Hagemann, 1996, 13).

Readers experience Welsh's 344-page novel as a series of forty-three "loosely connected" sections which are further organized into seven parts, each separated from the one before by a blank page, title-page, and another blank page: Kicking, Relapsing, Kicking Again, Blowing It, Exile, Home and Exit (plus in the US edition a useful but incomplete five page Glossary). It is this progression from Kicking to clearly marked Exit that the book's Contents announces and foregrounds, in sharp contrast to the actual reading experience which, except briefly as the reader moves from one of the seven parts to the next, seems far more discontinuous. The semblance of progression and continuity that the seven-part organization and the Contents pages create was especially emphasized for readers (and therefore reviewers) of the original 1993 Secker & Warburg edition, who, even before reaching the Contents, would have had the op-portunity to read the teaser, printed on the inside cover:

Mark Renton is a very sick young man. He's sick of heroin and sick of trying to get off it. He's also sickened by what he sees around him in the AIDS capital of Europe: forgotten housing schemes, derelict docklands and ignorant bigotry. Above all, Renton is thoroughly sick of himself. Surrounded by friends like the exploitative Sick Boy, the psychopathic Begbie and the thieving, feline-obsessed Spud, the last thing Renton needs is enemies, but he's finding out that the old cliché about your own worst enemy has more than a ring of truth. What with vampire ghost babies, exploding siblings, disastrous sexual encounters and the Hibs' worst season ever, it's plain to see why Renton gloomily contends that "life does not get any easier."

In trying to anticipate and mitigate objections to *Trainspotting*'s "ramshackle" structure by positing a central character and a strong plot line, this teaser does not so much misrepresent Welsh's novel as it misrepresents the reader's experience of it—in Welsh's own words, "the process of how people engage with it" (Reynolds, 1998, 11). It is a process Welsh likened to the way clubbers respond to house music and how in general they have learned to respond to their overstimulated environment of advertising and soundbites, music videos, computer graphics, etc. To write for such an audience, whose way of processing information has been transformed by their technologically enhanced environment, the writer has to have something happen on every page, "to keep the pages turning, to keep the action moving, just like a DJ" (Smith, L. C., 1996). "You just get into the rhythm of it and, once you do that, it doesn't really matter how the words are written on the page" (Bresnark, 1999). What does matter is "the constant motion and movement" that Welsh found so appealing about Danny Boyle's first film, *Shallow Grave* and that makes *Trainspotting* so "pacy, punchy, state of the era," as *i-D* magazine said of one of the numerous anthologies (*Children of Albion Rovers*) which *Trainspotting* helped spawn and in which Welsh's writing appeared. To talk about *Trainspotting*'s structure or, more precisely, to complain of its formal deficiencies, may be beside the point in so far as structure here may be irrelevant, as outdated in the postmodern world as metanarratives, the absence of which is one of the defining characteristics of what Jean-Francis Lyotard calls the "postmodern condition." Perhaps we should say not that *Trainspotting* is structureless but that it is differently structured—and in fact intensely aware of the artifice and arbitrariness of all structuring systems, systems that Welsh exposes and parodies, offering up decrowning doubles and alternative structuring devices. This self-consciousness about the artifice of structure is apparent on the novel's first page in Mark's commentary on the formulaic nature of Jean-Claude Van Damme films, with their "obligatory dramatic opening" and "building up the tension through introducing the dastardly villain and sticking the weak plot thegither" (3). Mark is similarly aware of the various games played off-screen as well: humiliation games, grieving games, reminiscing games and of course the giro schemes in which Mark is involved.

More interesting are the structuring devices Welsh deploys as alternatives to the metastructures of plot, character, nationalism, etc. as he presents his "series of inter-echoing vignettes." There are the weak, tenuous causal connections between sections and the sporadic appearances of what we might call tertiary characters such as Sutherland, mentioned just three times in the entire narrative (once early, twice late), whose reappearance helps create a sense of coherence (and, in Sutherland's case, menace). And there are the recurrent images, such as Spud's grandmother's varicose veins (123) and the "varicose-vein flats, called so because of the plastered cracks all over its facing" (315). More pervasive are the eyes (e.g., "nothing in his [Sick Boy's] eyes but need" [4], eyes that just five pages and one hit of heroin later are "now innocent and full ay wonder" [9], and so nothing like the eyes Iggy Pop trains on Tommy (and others) during the Barrowlands concert or what passes between Mark and Tommy at the end of "Winter in West Granton" when their eyes meet. Then there are all the brothers, who contribute to both the novel's realism and its portrayal of Leith's complex power grid.

The deployment of parallel scenes and narrative lines also serves to make *Trainspotting* more coherent than it seems. Upon learning that his son is HIV-positive, Davie Mitchell's father at first says nothing but later that night arrives at his son's flat, tearfully embracing "my laddie." Soon after, in an otherwise unrelated scene/section, an unidentified old drunk "considers saying something [to Spud or any one of the other young men who come in with him, whom the old man thinks may be one of his many carelessly conceived biological offspring], before deciding that he has nothing to say to him" (264). Later still, another, or perhaps the same, old drunk does say something to Mark and Begbie, who is the old man's son, though neither acknowledges this fact. The robbery Begbie and Spud commit at a DIY and Begbie's mistreatment of the boy who made the robbery possible parallels the London drug dealer Peter Gilbert's subsequent treatment of Begbie and the others, whom Gilbert "straight away . . . clocks . . . as small-time wasters who have stumbled on a big deal" who end up selling their dope for £2000 less than were prepared to take and £1000 less than Gilbert was prepared to offer. Minor characters not only reappear, the way Sutherland does; they circulate among vignettes. Spud, for example, is interested in Nicola Hanson but leaves the gathering with Alison; Matty later gets a kitten from Nicola to give to his daughter Lisa, but Lisa's mother, Matty's former girlfriend, rejects the gift, which Matty then keeps but does not care for; the litterbox overflows with cat excrement and urine, causing the taxoplasmosis which kills Matty, which in turn leads to Matty's funeral and "Memories of Matty," in which his friends and relatives remember him in decidedly non-elegaic ways (bad in bed, lousy guitarist, wimpy mate, irresponsible father). Matty may be a secondary character (or less) but the novel's main narrative lines take place against the background, or bass beat, of his decline: "something's wrong with Matty," 153; Matty is in hospital, 176; Matty is dead, 286, not as a result of the usual AIDS complications, but of shit-induced taxo-plasmosis. A seemingly minor character in "Her Man," whose name is mentioned only in passing and as (or as if as) an afterthought, becomes a central figure in "Bad Blood," *Trainspotting*'s longest section.

Sudden swerves in the narrative, not just between the forty-three sections but within them as well, between paragraphs, even sentences, help create *Trainspotting*'s particular rhythm. Those disruptions are more noticeable and have attracted a good deal of attention from reviewers and others who have tried to understand the ways in which *Trainspotting* "moderate[s] between black comedy, anger, farce and tragedy" ("Bard"), "juggles sincerity and cynicism, ennui and energy, fashionable despair and smarmy sentimentality" (Roberts, 1996), and "swerves between wit, anger, cynicism, and unexpected tenderness" (Lasdun, 1996), at times in accordance with whatever drug a character has just ingested, injected or inserted. Certain of these startling juxtapositions derive from Welsh's quick-cutting: Renton seeing the young "woman" he had sex with the previous night metamorphose into the fourteen year old school girl who looks twelve without makeup, sixteen with, and ten when walking hand-in-hand with Renton ("twenty-five going on forty" but suddenly feeling a doubly vulnerable stoat-the-baw fifty-five). The description of Sick Boy and Alison quoted earlier that ends so idyllically with "baith look[ing] strangely beautiful and pure in the flickering candlelight," for example, is immediately followed by Ali's "That beats any meat injection . . . that beats any fuckin cock in the world." One section ends with Stevie and Stella, who has just arrived from London on New Year's eve, kissing; the next begins with Lesley screaming, having just discovered that her baby is dead in her crib. A quarter-century before, Vonnegut would have added "So it goes"; Welsh adds nothing. Another section ends with Mark's brother Billy and others booting a former mate; the next, about

Mark's efforts to free himself from heroin, is titled "Kicking Again." The repose of "Searching for the Inner Man" is followed by a frantic Renton trying to figure out how he ended up under "House Arrest" in his parents flat, forced into withdrawal after a nearly fatal overdose. Certain of these juxtapositions are foregrounded and obvious: the Begbie "myths" and "reality" (82–83) or the official eulogies for Billy and Matty and the unspoken, unofficial thoughts of the mourners. Other juxtapositions are more subtle. After the gross revenge comedy of "Eating Out," the grimness and mournfulness of "Trainspotting at Leith Central Station," set during the "festive period" of Christmas, is intensified by the fact that none of the people seen exiting the theater after a performance of *Carmen* seem any more interested in or even aware of the real life street drama going on around them than the four Englishmen are of Kelly's revenge. Other connections seem not so much more subtle as just more postmodern: for example, the hyperlink, as it were, that connects the mention of Begbie at the end of one section with his first person narration in the next.

"Trainspotting at Leith Central Station" also makes use of another structuring device that significantly contributes to the novel's overall sense of bleakness and constriction: sections which come full circle, ending where they began and thus creating a sense not of completion and closure but of futility and constraint. It is more obviously present in "London Crawling," which ends as it began, with Mark feeling intensely alone and repeating the same line at section's end that he had used near the beginning ("We are all slags oan hoaliday"). But it is used even more effectively in "Trainspotting at Leith Central Station." The section begins noting the high probability that anyone going down Leith Walk at that time of night will be assaulted, then Mark meeting up with a drunken friend who nearly does assault him before Renton can put him in a taxi and send him on his way home; Mark next meets up with Begbie, who makes him feel less a potential victim and "pathetic arsehole" and more the predator; they then meet the old drunk, whom Mark soon realizes is Begbie's father. At this point, someone is assaulted—no one in particular, just a handy outlet for Begbie's frustration and rage. This time around, Begbie's habitual frustration and rage are deepened, perhaps activated, by the resentful psychopathic son's coming face-to-face with his pathetic and irresponsible father (one of *Trainspotting*'s many pathologically deadbeat dads; Begbie is another). "The expression the guy had when he looked up at Begbie was mair one ay resignation than fear. The boy understood everything." And so does Mark, who has chosen not to intervene, "even in a token way," and who walks off with Begbie, "neither ay us looking back once" (309). This closing of the circle is in a way even more troubling than the various narrative disruptions mentioned earlier—linguistic, tonal, structural.

The fact that *Trainspotting* is mainly narrated in the first person and in the form of interior monologues of characters who are immersed in their subcultures contributes to the novel's paradoxical effect: its feeling at once fragmented, even "ramshackle," yet oddly coherent and of a piece. Welsh's authorial detachment—the refusal to judge, along with the absence of bourgeois "misrepresentation" and "voyeuristic intrusion" (Welsh, "Welcome")—helped ensure *Trainspotting*'s success even as it led cultural commentators to deplore what they believed was either Welsh's "lack of moral engagement" or, worse, his endorsement of junkie lowlife. Concerned with consequences rather than with causes, with depicting rather than either castigating or approving, with a measure of sympathetic understanding for characters presented from within rather than from on high, *Trainspotting* chooses to allow its characters to speak for themselves in their own voices without apology and without much hope of being heard by the judges, counselors, employment officers paid to listen.

SETTING

Before taking up the novel's characters, I want to turn briefly to the
novel's setting and Welsh's handling of time and place. With few
exceptions (Tommy and Mitch's trip to Glasgow for the Iggy Pop
concert and Mark's trips to London), *Trainspotting* is set entirely in
Edinburgh. But the Edinburgh of the novel is not the Edinburgh
of the Fodor's-fueled popular imagination. It is not the Edinburgh
of high teas, Scottish history, and the Edinburgh Festival. It is,
rather, an Edinburgh that lies well beyond the festival's official
Fringe, well north of the gentrified city center, between the postwar
housing schemes of Muirhouse to the west and the rundown docklands of Leith (subsequently undergoing its own gentrification) to
the east. Thus the rude discovery made by Monny's aunt. She
arrives in Edinburgh from an island off the West Coast of Ireland,
sees what any tourist sees—"the castle n Princes Street, n the High
Street"—and, thinking "the whole fuckin place wis like that," sub-
mits her application at the Housing Office where, after it has been
treated by the staff with the requisite degree of contempt and deri-
sion, she finds herself in "one ay they hoatline joabs in West Granton, thit nae cunt else wants. Instead ay a view ay the castle, she's
goat a view ay the gasworks" (115). The specificity with which
Welsh sketches the urban setting—streets, pubs, clubs, parks, public
buildings, shopping precincts and bus routes—contributes to the
novel's realism. But there is more to Welsh's setting than that. His
slice of Edinburgh life is the decrowning double not just of the city
of tourists but of "the Edinburgh virtues of hard work, respectability
and godliness"; the world according to Welsh is a place of unem-
ployment, giro schemes, scruffiness, alcoholism, violence, drugs,
prostitution, and the God of "Granton Star Cause" (in *The Acid
House*), a mean-spirited old drunk.

Although place is handled quite specifically in *Trainspotting*, time is not. "If you want to be pedantic about it," Welsh has said of the novel's historical moment, "you could say it was set in Edinburgh between 1982 and 1988, but the issues of drug addiction and drug abuse and the on-going HIV issues are as pertinent as ever — probably more so now" (Macdonald, 1996). The six year period coincides with the sudden influx of cheap heroin into the city, the attendant dramatic increase in the rate of HIV infection, and the time that the ravages of both were impressing themselves on Welsh during his several returns to Leith from London, just as one phase of contemporary British history drew to a close and another was born. Which is to say, just as punk gave way to rave and club culture. In fact, however, *Trainspotting* begins and ends a bit later than Welsh remembered and takes place over a shorter period too, though not as short as the year or so that readers may assume. "Back in 1985," "the shooting galleries which flourished . . . in the mid-eighties" and the "twenty years" which have elapsed since Davie Mitchell's father last attended a soccer match (1970) help orient the reader, as, to a certain extent, do the novel's few, and invariably undated, mentions of actual events. Assuming that the action, such as it is, is essentially continuous, we can date it as beginning sometime before Iggy Pop's Barrowlands concert (15 December 1988) and ending at the time of the Pogues' gig at the Fleadh staged in Finsbury Park (2 December 1991), a time when Mandela's release from prison and the Sandanista's defeat at the polls (both February 1990) were already too *passé* to work to Sick Boy's sexual advantage but memories of the Falklands War (1982) and news of the future transfer of Hong Kong from Britain to China (agreed to in 1984 and effected in 1997) were still fresh — the first to enable the one-legged Johnny Swan to pose as a wounded veteran and the second to prompt a racist rant from Davie Mitchell's father as he reads the *Evening News*.

Drugs (heroin and speed, not yet ecstasy, at least not much) and music serve as other ways of noting passing time. In addition to Iggy Pop, there are references to "the Ziggy Stardust era Bowie," the Simple Minds' abandoning their "pomp-rock roots" for U2-style "passion rock." Socio-economic changes manifest themselves in similarly culture-specific ways; the London real estate boom, for example, evidences itself in the transformation of a bar Mark liked to patronize into "a frighteningly sanitized hole" for yuppie City wannabes. Welsh's handling of the passage of time in his characters' lives is similarly, and appropriately, vague. Within the overall "progress" indicated by the novel's seven-part structure (from Kicking to Exit), the passage of time occurs in fits and starts that greatly distort the reader's sense of duration and continuity. The novel's first four sections take place in August at the time of the Edinburgh Festival. On the novel's second page, Mark and Sick Boy find getting a taxi difficult: "up cruising fat, rich festival cunts too fuckin lazy tae walk a hundred fuckin yards fae one poxy church hall tae another fir thir fuckin show." Following the brief "Junk Dilemmas No. 63," the next section takes place, as its title indicates, on "The First Day of the Edinburgh Festival," a day incidentally, just as hot as the one earlier (the day before?) had been cold (which is not a slip on Welsh's part, just a meteorological fact of Edinburgh life). The next section also takes place during the Festival, as Sick Boy tries to pick up two young Festival-goers. The section after that, "Growing Up in Public," takes place at the time of Nina's period and during "the strange festival of grief" that follows her Uncle Andy's sudden death. Whether this "strange festival of grief" takes place at the time of the Edinburgh Festival or sometime after (or even before) is not made clear. The exact time of the next section is made clear, again in its title: "Victory on New Year's Day." To sum up: the first four sections/thirty pages take place over just a few days. The next two sections/eleven pages, each covering just a few hours, move the action ahead four full months. Complicating matters still more is the fact that temporal markers such as Edinburgh Festival, August, New Year's, "the festive season of Christmas," and so forth are quite rare, as are another kind of temporal marker: for example, Spud is sentenced to ten months in prison on p. 168 and reported to have just been released on p. 211, allowing the reader to assume that ten months have passed over these forty-three pages — the same ten months between the time Mark's brother Billy reenlists (reported on pp. 132 and 171) and the time he is killed (p. 210) at Crossmaglen, the "Border village with the fearsome reputation," as the *Times* puts it.

Far more significant about the novel's handling of time is the way it creates a sense of immediacy and thereby contributes or reflects the "weakening of historicity, both in our relationship to public History and in the new forms of our private temporality," that Fredric Jameson has identified as characteristic of postmodernism and "the cultural logic of late capitalism" (1991, 6). Welsh divides his 344-page novel into forty-three "loosely connected" sections (for an average of eight pages per section, though a few are less than a page and others up to twenty four pages). Less noticeable but arguably more effective in creating the sense that the characters are living in and we are reading about an endless present and the sense of disconnection and dislocation associated with it is the way Welsh handles verb tense. Not surprisingly, most of *Trainspotting* is narrated in the present tense. But even those sections, paragraphs and sentences narrated in the past slip into (and sometimes back out of) the present without notice and with dismaying ease, thus blurring the distinction between these two time codes so that, as in film, scenes and events revisited narratively are relived and therefore experienced in the present, without the distance and therefore assurance and at least relative closure that the past tense connotes.

Contributing to the sense of immediacy are the popular cultural reference points ranging only as far back as the 1960s-early 1970s — Carly Simon, David Bowie, and Lou Reed — but more often dealing with more recent popular music. As we just saw, references to contemporary historical events and issues outside the realm of popular culture are both infrequent and undated. Those to high culture are similarly rare: the high-toned Edinburgh Festival which exists on *Trainspotting*'s fringe, the opera *Carmen* mentioned earlier, Kierkegaard, Brecht, brief parodies of Dickens's *A Christmas Carol* ("and god bless the NHS"), Shakespeare's *Hamlet* ("*Alas poor Alan, I knew him Nurse. He was a wanker and an infinite pest*") and perhaps *MacBeth* ("We aw live, then we die, in quite a short space ay time n aw. That's it; end ay fuckin story"). Further down the cultural ladder we find the ballad "A Scottish Soldier" and the writer H. P. Lovecraft ("Nazi cunt . . . but he spun a good yarn"). Contemporary popular culture dominates: not just the music mentioned above, but cinema (Sean Connery's James Bond films, Roger Moore [a later Bond], Lee Marvin, Charles Bronson, Jean-Claude Van Damme, Michael J. Fox, porn films, *The Accused, The Wizard of Oz*) and, on television, *Coronation Street, The Generation Game* and of course football. These mentions serve not only to flesh out the characters' world and the novel's realism in much the same way that the mention of actual parks, pubs and streets do. They also allow the characters to create idealized as well as temporary identities and escapist fantasies for themselves (Sick Boy as another Edinburgh boy, Sean Connery, as Special Agent 007, James Bond; Renton as James Cagney as well as the footballer Alec MacLeish) and ways to understand one another (as when Mark uses another cinematic reference to undermine Begbie's self-aggrandizing "Ah'm fackin Lee Marvin" — rhyming slang for "starving" — by saying Begbie in fact looks "like an arrogant aristocrat finding himself in reduced circumstances.")

CHARACTERS

In accepting the Booker Prize in 1994, James Kelman declared, "My culture and my language have the right to exist and no one has the authority to dismiss that" (Walsh, 1996). Minus the well-intentioned but high-flown nationalist sentiment, the same may be said of *Trainspotting*, whose language and characters form its "major dynamic" (Paget, 1999, 132). Although some have complained that Welsh (like Kelman) "presents the Scots as the English like to see them: drunken or drugged, aggressive, illiterate, socially inept, boorish" (Gordon, 1997), Welsh is at least partly playing off this stereotype, that is, "the gendered figuration of the Caledonian as a wild man, operating beyond the bounds of normal civilization" (Crawford, 2000, 331). His "mob of resolutely nihilistic characters" (Jolly) are the (then) largely unrepresented Scottish, or more specifically Reekie, equivalents of the title figure of Ken Coates's *The Forgotten Englishmen*, one of the very few works that Welsh has acknowledged as an influence. Admittedly, Welsh depicts his (then) unconventional cast in unconventional ways that border on or topple over into caricature, not unlike the grotesques of Sherwood Anderson's *Winesburg, Ohio*, which concerns the differently stultifying life in an American Midwestern town. As with Anderson, Welsh's caricatures yield insight, making his often unlikable characters understandable. They are people "whose ideals and ambitions," Welsh has said, "perhaps outstrip what society has to offer them," but who nonetheless possess "a real will to survive" (Macdonald, 1996; Bahr, 2000). If, as Mick Brown has pointed out, the British youth culture of teddy boys, mods and rockers, punks and ravers is "traditionally tribal" and "all about belonging," then much of what proves so disturbing about *Trainspotting* is the absence of nearly any benefit accruing from belonging to the Leith subculture.

Welsh's presentation of his "graphic, outsize characters" individualizes them to an almost intolerable degree.

As with any novel having a large cast, *Trainspotting*'s characters may be divided according to degree of importance to the overall narrative based in part on frequency and duration of appearance. At one extreme are those who are merely mentioned or who have a small, clearly definable function to perform (taxi drivers, bartenders, judges, therapists, Andreas, Festival-goers and other tourists, Begbie's victims) or who function as human furniture ("the fat sow" whom Mark encounters in "The First Day of the Edinburgh Festival"). Then there are those who appear once, sometimes twice, and at some length and who have an expanded but nonetheless localized role to play: the London drug-dealer Peter Gilbert, Spud's grandmother Na Na and his Uncle Dode, Mark's first shag in ages Dianne, Alan Venters, Mark's cousin Nina. Then there are the characters who circulate through the novel and thereby create the sense of a wider and more fully realized but nonetheless still severely circumscribed world: Stevie, for example, but more importantly Alison, Laura McEwan, Kelly (of "Eating Out" and "The Elusive Mr Hunt") who are parts of Mark's social world; Tommy's friend Davie Mitchell (of "Traditional Sunday Breakfast" and "Bad Blood") who exists on its fringe; and Mark's parents and brother Billy. Then there is the inner circle of Welsh's *Inferno*: Begbie, Sick Boy, Spud, Tommy and Renton. Mark is, of course, the novel's central character, though he occupies that position in a very different way than Pip does in *Great Expectations* or Jay Gatsby (or Nick Carraway) in *The Great Gatsby* or Stephen Dedalus (or Leopold Bloom) in *Ulysses*. Oddly enough, Mark is a central character only in the dispersed sporadic way that Nick Shay is in Don DeLillo's *Underworld*.

But to classify the characters solely in terms of this kind of narrative importance is to obscure other ways that may prove equally

illuminating: drug user/non-user, employed/unemployed, criminal/
non-criminal, violent/non-violent, male/female. One especially interesting difference between the male characters, that are the novel's
ostensible focus, and the female, whose number turns out to be
surprisingly large, has to do with naming. The women are conven-
tionally named: Alison, Kelly, June, Sharon, Stella, Carol, Hazel,
Laura McEwan, Gail Hudson. The central and secondary male
characters, on the other hand, are multiply named, with the names
often indicating the various groups and subcultures to which the
characters belong and their roles and degree of power within those
subcultures. Mark Renton is Mark, Renton, Rents and (worst) the
Rent Boy ("ma semen-rectumed chum"). Johnny Swan, one of
Mark's close boyhood friends, now his dealer of choice, is Swanney,
the White Swan and Mother Superior "because ay the length ay
time he'd hud his habit." The part names play in the novel's power
grid is especially noticeable when necessity forces Mark to buy from
another dealer, Mike Forrester: he's Mike when Rents has to be
deferential but Forry once Mark has the drugs and the balance of
power has shifted. To some extent this includes the balance of
power between novel and reader as the latter tries to familiarize
him- or herself with the former and its multiply named characters;
for example, Ricky/Monny/Richard Monaghan; Rab McLaughlin,
aka Secks, short for Second Prize, a nickname left unexplained
until the novel's final pages.

Vonnegut liked to point out that death is a convenient way for
writers to get rid of minor characters. Deciding on a main character
may be just as convenient. Although Mark Renton is indeed
Welsh's main character, the novel's structure means that the reader
can never enjoy the luxury of either forgetting the other characters
or subordinating their stories and voices to Mark's narrative. They
are not merely his mates nor are they simply foils who enable us to
understand Mark's strengths and weaknesses better. None is Laertes

(to Mark's Hamlet) nor was meant to be. Rather they are like those unstillable voices in Beckett, clamoring to be heard. There is Spud (Danny Murphy, variously described as "gentle, laid-back" and "lazy, scruffy"; according to Mark "a classic acid-heid by temperament," according to Sick Boy someone with an "effortless ability to transform the most innocent of pastimes into criminality. . . . Even in his Ma's womb, you would have had to define Spud less as a foetus, more as a set of dormant drug and personality problems" (328). He is also linguistically the novel's most easily recognizable character. Even as his utterances, liberally sprinkled with "ken" and "likesay," suggest his intellectual limitations, his equally characteristic rhyming slang suggests something quite different. The same can be said about the comical misadventures that make up Spud's sex life, the flip side of a sad and desperate loneliness that makes him one of the novel's most sympathetic characters, as well as one with the fewest resources and prospects, only a step up from the even bleaker futures faced by his half-black Uncle Dode or his HIV-positive friend Tommy.

Sick Boy (Simon David Williams, Si, Simone) is everything Spud is not. "They call um Sick Boy, no because he's eywis sick wi junk withdrawal, but because he's just one sick cunt" (3): handsome, obsessed with Sean Connery/James Bond, ready to exploit and betray his mates and pimp out his numerous girlfriends. "The socialists go on about your comrades, your class, your union, and society. Fuck all that shite. The Tories go on about your employer, your country, your family. Fuck that even mair. It's me, me, fucking ME, SIMON DAVID WILLIAMSON, NUMERO FUCKING UNO, versus the world, and it's a one-sided swedge" (30). High on himself, he doesn't need drugs and is able to quit almost at will. Overcoming his addiction to "get[ting] off with a woman and her purse" proves much harder. Tommy is different, preferring speed to heroin or greed and "addicted to having sex" with one woman only, Lizzie MacIntosh — "a shag extraordinaire" with "a tongue like a sailor and a castrating stare" — to any one else, until, that is, he chooses buying a ticket to the Iggy Pop concert instead of buying Lizzie a birthday present. He loses Lizzie, takes up heroin, soon becomes HIV-positive and is last seen living alone in one of the varicose vein flats out in West Granton, the once super-fit Tommy now a handy target for schemie kids with nothing better to do than menace an HIVer.

Francis Begbie — Franco, the General, the Beggar, Hurricane Franco — is the novel's most menacing character, his entire person-ality boiled down to the opposite of Spud's terminal passivity. Begbie is violence in its purest and most gratuitous form. Although he avoids drugs and rails against them with all the fervor of the Just Say No crowd, Begbie is addicted to alcohol and to violence in all forms. His idea of a good time is pubcrawling, stealing, discerning slights and provocations where there are none, and causing may-hem, glassing, stabbing, and/or booting the impotent and unsus-pecting. Not even his pregnant girlfriend is spared his wrath: "Nae cunt gits fuckin lippy wi me, bairn or nae fuckin bairn." He terrifies the mates whom he claims to protect and who, while boosting his ego, know that Begbie "is like junk, a habit" and that his "temper could send them all to prison for life." Indeed it is thinking about Begbie that sends Mark off on one his best remembered outbursts:

Ah hate cunts like that. Cunts like Begbie. Cunts that are intae baseball-batting every fucker that's different; pakis, poofs, n what huv ye. Fuckin failures in a country ay failures. It's nae good blamin it oan the English fir colonising us. Ah don't hate the English. They're just wankers. We are colonised by wankers. We can't even pick a decent, vibrant, healthy culture to be colonised by. No. We're ruled by effete arseholes. What does that make us? The lowest of the fuckin low, the scum of the earth. The most wretched, servile, miserable, pathetic trash that was ever shat intae creation. Ah don't hate the English. They just git oan wi the shite thuv goat. Ah hate the Scots. (78)

In a novel in which, as Kasia Boddy has noted, "no single narrative is allowed to dominate," Mark Renton is, if not *Trainspotting*'s "linguistic epicentre" (Skinner, 1999, 219), then at the very least a character whose recurrent presence, overall trajectory, and relative, even ambiguous victory gives Welsh's text a coherence and sense of "purpose" it would otherwise lack and against which the other voices clamoring to be heard do not so much revolve as take on added resonance. We must not overestimate Renton's success, however. His is not the unambiguous, quasi-spiritual redemption of the heroin addict and convicted fratricide Ezekiel Farragut in John Cheever's *Falconer* (1977), who escapes first his addiction, then his prison, ready to take his place as he rightly saw it, having "lost his fear of falling and all other fears of that nature. He held his head high, his back straight, and walked along nicely. Rejoice, he thought, rejoice." Renton may or may not be on the road to secular redemption; he is however on the run from those he both resembles and differs from. What especially sets him apart (aside from the fact that more of the novel focuses on him than on any other single character) is his being more observant and self-conscious and self-critical, as well as less prone to self-deception, than most, maybe all, of those around him. He is certainly the most linguistically resourceful and the one with the fewest illusions and self-delusions. To call him "an intellectual raver" (Peter, 1995) and "an intellectual manque" (Self, 1996) only begins to get at why the judge who sentences Spud to prison as a habitual thief sends Renton to rehab, believing him "a different matter." He is someone who steals books to read them rather than just to support a drug habit, though not to read them as part of a program of self-improvement. Mark is too cynical for that, though he is not too cynical to recognize "real bravery" when he sees it (Davie Mitchell coming to Billy's funeral despite being HIV-positive) and to speak for those who no longer can, including Julie Mathieson:

Ah really liked Julie. . . . She wis a really good punter. She hud a bairn whin she wis HIV, but the bairn wis all-clear, thank fuck. The hoespital sent Julie hame in an ambulance wi the bairn, wi two guys dressed in sortay radioactive-proof suits—helmets, the lot. This wis back in 1985. It had the predictable effect. The neighbours saw this, freaked, and burnt her oot the hoose. Once ye git tagged HIV, that's you fucked. Especially a lassie oan her puff. Harassment followed harassment. Eventually, she hud a nervous breakdoon and, wi her damaged immune system, wis easy prey fir the onset ay AIDS. (78)

The details of Mark's life are easy enough to understand even if dispersed throughout the text. He is "twenty-five going on forty," his ginger hair dyed black and spiked, a Hibs fan and IV drug-user; Catholic mother, Protestant Glaswegian father, one older brother, Billy, one younger, the mentally and physically handicapped David, formerly institutionalized and now dead a year; a good student when doing well academically results in getting away from Begbie; otherwise unmotivated, he settles for much less: a certificate in joining followed by a half year at Aberdeen University, where he spends his education grant on drugs and prostitutes.

If his several attempts at drug withdrawal form the backbone of his and (at times less apparently) the novel's narrative, Mark's withdrawal from most social contacts—visiting friends, especially sick ones, and attending funerals—prove no less frequent and arguably even more troubling than his several returns to heroin. The novel in fact begins with Mark watching a video in his darkened Montgomery Street flat, trying to pay no heed to his importunate friend, Sick Boy, who desperately needs a fix. Eventually Mark accompanies Sick Boy, but only after realizing that soon he too will need his own fix. Once that's been secured, Mark heads straight back to his flat and his rented video, "gleefully anticipat[ing] the stomping he's [Jean-Claude Van Damme] gaunnae gie that smart cunt" (13). It is a choice that means not visiting Kelly, still depressed following an abortion performed the week before. That Mark may have been responsible for Kelly's becoming pregnant is, of course, a possibility he quickly rationalizes away, leaving him free to watch the video and Kelly to cope as best she can on her own. As Kelly later says, "Mark can be affectionate, but he doesnae seem tae really need people" (302). Indeed, while his cynicism is no less refreshing than his freedom from the fantasies of sex (Mother Superior), violence (Begbie) and being numero uno (Sick Boy) that fuel the dreams of many of the novel's no-hopers, Mark's lack of commitment or active concern is disturbing. He may have preferences, but he has few principles. He is a vegetarian solely because he does not like meat. In fact, he dislikes most everything and everyone other than his "beautiful heroine": cats, dogs, Wedgies, speed, everyone at and everything about Aberdeen University, Scots no less than the English, and both Labour and the Tories (though in this last Mark sounds very much like Welsh himself).

Although in a sense Mark's dislikes are as indiscriminate as Begbie's violence, there is something to be said for both the venom and vehemence with which he turns Nancy Reagan's famous, and famously ineffective, solution to the "drug problem" — "Just say no" — on its head in his own now equally famous Choose Life rap:

Society invents a spurious convoluted logic tae absorb and change people whae's behaviour is outside its mainstream. Suppose that ah ken aw the pros and cons, know that ah'm gaunnae huv a short life, am ay sound mind etcetera, etcetera, but still want tae use smack? They won't let ye dae it. They won't let ye dae it, because it's seen as ah sign ay thir ain failure. The fact that ye jist simply choose tae reject whit they huv tae offer. Choose us. Choose life. Choose mortgage payments; choose washing machines; choose cars; choose sitting oan a couch watching mind-numbing and spirit-crushing game shows, stuffing fuckin junk food intae yir mooth. Choose rotting away, pishing and shiteing yersel in a home, a total fuckin embarrassment tae the selfish, fucked-up brats ye've produced. Choose life.

Well, ah choose no tae choose life. If the cunts cannae handle that, it's thair fuckin problem. (187–188)

Mark is partially defined in terms of what he is not and who he is not (as violent and self-deluded as Begbie, as passive as Spud, as sick as Tommy, as narcissistic as Sick Boy) and in terms of what he rejects, including ready-made national identities:

Ah've never felt British, because ah'm not. It's ugly and artificial. Ah've never really felt Scottish either, though. Scotland the brave, ma arse; Scotland the shitein cunt. We'd throttle the life oot ay each other fir the privilege ay rimmin some English aristocrat's piles. Ah've never felt a fuckin thing aboot countries, other than total disgust. They should abolish the fuckin lot ay them. Kill every fuckin parasite politician that ever stood up and mouthed lies and fascist platitudes in a suit and a smarmy smile. (228)

And while the intensity of his rejections is disturbing, verbally violent, it seems entirely appropriate, a Herculean as well as Swiftian-Rabelaisian cleansing action, stripping away all "the boring middle-class shite," political platitudes and the ad-speak of Choose Life campaigns (whether against drugs or abortion or for, in Bill Clinton's well-spun phrase, "growing the economy"). Often (but not always), Mark is nearly as hard on himself, especially whenever

he starts to pontificate, which he does when Tommy asks him what
heroin does for him (pp. 89–90). Mark goes on — half-rhapsodic,
half-avuncular — about heroin as an "honest drug," as a response to
life's disappointments, and as a way of both intensifying feelings and
anesthetizing oneself. When Tommy responds, "Shite," Mark has
to agree, at least to himself, acknowledging that he doesn't really
know why he uses heroin and that he'd probably give a different
answer were he asked the same question on another day. Thinking
about the matter further, he realizes that there are two less lofty
explanations for his using heroin. One has to do with commitment:

Ma problem is, whenever ah sense the possibility, or realise the actuality ay
attaining something that ah thought ah wanted, be it girlfriend, flat, job,
education, money and so on, it jist seems so dull n sterile, that ah cannae
value it any mair. Junk's different though. Ye cannae turn yir back oan it
sae easy. It willnae let ye. Trying tae manage a junk problem is the ultimate
challenge. (90)

The other is, "It's also a fuckin good kick." Significantly, he only
tells Tommy about the latter; the former is too private, too revealing,
too shameful.

Begbie acts without thinking and Sick Boy acts with malice
aforethought. Mark on the other hand does think and often feels
guilty about what he either does or does not do. Thus the "powerful
twinge of self-loathing" he feels when he thinks about having had
sex with fourteen year old Dianne — not that this keeps him from
having sex with her again, soon after that twinge. Or the compassion
he feels for his dead brother Billy's pregnant and abused girlfriend —
not that that compassion prevents him from hustling her on her
way when it's time for his next fix any more than it would have kept
him from shagging her earlier that day. And it is also there early in
the novel in however qualified a form in his "playing the man" for

Leslie, who has just found her baby dead. "The gadges move a few steps back and watch in silence as ah cook. The fuckers will huv tae wait. Lesley comes first, eftir me. That goes without saying" (56). Clearly here is a moral sense that is both ambiguously motivated (playing The Man, as much a social construct as a cinematic stereotype) and dismayingly limited, though still better than anything any of the other main (male) characters offer, including Mark much of the time, with his own preference for drug- and video-induced oblivion. This residual moral sense is also present in the ruefulness of Mother Superior's observation, "Nae friends in this game. Jist associates." It is an observation that Mark recalls soon after he and Sick arrive at the White Swan's and that he wants to repeat a few pages later to his friends: "it sounds good in ma heid: 'We are all acquaintances now.' It seems tae go beyond our personal junk circumstances; a brilliant metaphor for our times." But "Ah resist the temptation," fearful of being "singled oot fir visiting duties" (11) but fearful too, one suspects, of actually identifying and speaking what they all feel.

Against the backdrop of (1) this need for community which exists in *Trainspotting* in negative form and for commitment and intimacy that Mark too resists (especially evident in the his failed relationship with Kelly), (2) Mark's cycles of addiction and withdrawal, and (3) Begbie's escalating violence, Mark increasingly feels "the limitations and ugliness of this place" and the people in it. Others feel it too: Begbie, who also feels trapped by his friends; Sick Boy, who does manage to go to France for a while; and Kelly, who wants her university degree—"Ah really fuckin want it more than anything" (303). Other than brief stays in London, however, Mark does little to alter his worsening situation until he steals the £17,000 he, Spud, Begbie, Secks and Sick Boy made by selling their drugs to Peter Gilbert. The theft has irrevocable consequences that work in Mark's favor, forcing him to do what earlier he only vaguely contemplated, leaving his friends and his city behind forever. This follows the logic Welsh introduced in "Grieving and Mourning in Port Sunshine," in which Billy and his mates punish one of their own who has betrayed the group in a scam involving a dead mate, his widow, and some collectively owned club money. The fact that Mark feels the need to rationalize his betrayal suggests his Hamlet-like indecision as well as a sense of honor among Leith lowlifes. Rationalization eventually gives way to affirmation, though nothing like the lyrical one at the end of *Falconer* nor the one at the end of "Bad Blood." There well-educated, mild-mannered, HIV-positive, university-educated (degree in chemistry) Dave, his murder of Venters safely behind him, back with Donna and reconciled with his family, and wishing that he "hadn't waited so long to be a human being," declares, "Life is beautiful. I'm going to enjoy it, and I'm going to have a long life. I'll be what the medical staff call a long-term survivor. I just *know* that I will" (262). Couched as much in terms of rejection as of redemption, Mark's situation is *somewhat* less cliched, less fraught and less unconvincingly upbeat:

Renton had used Begbie, used him to burn his boats completely and utterly. It was Begbie who ensured he could never return. He had done what he wanted to do. He could now never go back to Leith, to Edinburgh, even to Scotland, ever again. There, he could not be anything other than he was. Now, free from them all, for good, he could be what he wanted to be. He'd stand or fall alone. This thought both terrified and excited him as he contemplated life in Amsterdam. (344)

THEMES

Read in terms of the bourgeois novel tradition, Mark's escape, like Farragut's, represents the triumph of the autonomous self, rendered in the quasi-religious, liberal-humanist language of spiritual salvation and secular self-improvement. (Such an interpretation requires that the reader either forget or at least discount the various ways in which the novel stacks the deck against change, at least as effected through the usual means of faith (Dianne), hope (Sharon), education (Kelly, Geoff, David Mitchell)—or television ("The flick of a switch. Thank god for the remote control handset," Mark cynically notes. "You can move into different worlds at the press of a button" [202].) Read politically, as indeed both text and context demand, Mark's escape proves a more complicated and ambiguous matter. Cairns Craig reads Mark's freedom and his earlier drug-dependency allegorically, in terms of the larger political economy. According to Craig, the novel reveals "a community of dependency—welfare-dependency, drug-dependency, money-dependency—which is the mirror image of the society of isolated, atomized individuals of modern capitalism" based on "the dialectic of the fearful and the fearless," e.g., the fearful Renton and the pathologically fearless Begbie (97).

Read this way, Renton's great escape is not even the relative triumph it first seems. Rather, it is based on the continuation of that dialectic in a Scotland marked by the failure of the 1979 referendum and the fearfulness it expressed. Craig's reading of *Trainspotting* in relation to the referendum and the Scottish culture of political, economic, and cultural dependency is compelling and illuminating but nonetheless downplays a feature of Welsh's novel that is also characteristic of much contemporary Scottish writing, the sense of closure and containment that compels Mark's escape. This "desire to leave it all behind," as Boddy calls it (366), is intimately tied to the "dreams of emigration" that loom so large in *Marabou Stork Nightmares* and that, as Welsh has said, are "such a major part of Scottish working-class culture" (Smith, C. L., 1995). These "dreams of emigration" are distantly but significantly related to what Welsh most admires about Trocchi: his being "an internationalist and empowering figure for a lot of writers trying to escape the shackles of Scottishness, whose vision wasn't constrained by other people's definitions of Scottishness" ("A Scottish George Best of Literature," 1997, 17–18). Mark Renton does not go forth as Joyce's Stephen Dedalus does at the end of *Portrait of the Artist as a Young Man*, to "forge in the smithy of my soul, the uncreated conscience of my race," even if the language, rendered, significantly, both in standard English and the third person, does seem self-consciously and therefore ironically a bit high-flown and therefore false. Mark goes forth, by ferry, free of narrow notions such as race and nation, ready (as Welsh's subsequent work suggests) to take his place in the club culture where Ecstasy, not anti-social heroin, is the drug of choice.

But this means jumping ahead without first fully considering what Mark's fear of reprisal entails. If it serves as the measure of his social conscience before stepping off into the brave new world of competitive capitalism that the novel's closing paragraph suggests no less strongly than club-culture camaraderie and E-fuelled social revolution, it also indicates the heavy burden of Scots Presbyterian guilt and shame from which Mark has not yet freed himself. One can make the same argument about Welsh. The "dionysian energy" of his scatalogical prose and "the Welsh myth" of drink and drugs, punk and rave, may serve as "a defense against shame, not a liberation from it" (Adamson and Clark, 1999, 16), and therefore as a link between Welsh's anti-art and the consummate artistry of contemporary writers working more obviously with the theme of Scottish guilt, Janice Galloway and A. L. Kennedy. In addition to guilt and shame, Mark's exile, especially as couched in hyper-individualistic, Thatcher-like terms, is so striking in large part because of the desire for community that has formed one of the novel's most important subtexts. As we have seen, the heroin subculture is nearly as profoundly and self-destructively anti-social as the drug itself. Here even more than in *Naked Lunch*, we find Burroughs' "algebra of need" and the clear evidence that the drug economy is capitalism in its purest and most lethal form. Following much the same Orwellian logic that, as Barbara Ehrenreich once pointed out, makes divorce good, for the economy that is, in that it effectively forces people who when married shared a home, a television, a refrigerator, sofa, bed, etc., to have at least two of everything, IV-drug use, after AIDS, makes "positive" (as in HIV-positive) negative and "sharing" (and other forms of intimacy) dangerous to the user's health: risky personal behavior that requires government warnings.

Yet it is the longing to share, in its non-lethal form—"jist huvn somebody," as Tommy puts it just after breaking up with Lizzie and just before using heroin for the first time—that adds a certain poignancy to an otherwise alternately brutal and blackly humorous novel. Even Sick Boy, the ultimate narcissist, feels this need, playing the parts of both Sean Connery hero and rapt moviegoer-like audience. And so does Begbie, who recreates community in his own coercive image. But Spud, Mark, and Tommy are the male characters who experience this need and feel the absence of community most intensely. That Mark should feel this way while in London is not surprising (though it is ironic, given the equal intensity of his desire to leave Edinburgh behind). But he feels it in Leith as well. During the celebration that follows his successful court appearance, he thinks, "Ah'm surrounded by the cunts thit ur closest tae us; but ah've nivir felt so alone. Nivir in ma puff" (175). The old drunk in the pub in "There's a Light that Never Goes Out" and the other (?) old drunk who turns out to be Begbie's father, in "Trainspotting at Leith Central Station," are the iconic representations of this loneliness (as well as of a waste process that heroin did not cause, only exacerbated). They are what Mark—"twenty-five going on forty"—is fast becoming. Even those who are HIV-positive fail to "share" even during group meetings; instead they splinter: junkies resenting gays, whom they blame for bringing AIDS to Edinburgh, and straights resenting junkies and gays alike. Outside the group the situation is even worse for someone like Tommy who lacks the financial resources and family support of more affluent HIVers such as Davie Mitchell or Derek Jarman. As Mark explains, "His friends will decline in their numbers as his needs increase. The inverse, or perverse, mathematics ay life" (315–316).

Further ironizing this failure of community is the fact that, after pubs, drug dens, shooting galleries and the abandoned hulk of Leith Central Station, funerals serve as the most prevalent site of social interaction, albeit not of the cohesive kind. The number of the novel's dead and dying is as staggering as its mood of "menacing mortality." Reading *Trainspotting* is very much like what Luis Bunuel said it was like growing up in Lower Aragon, "Death was ever present, as in the Middle Ages." The dead and the dying, along with a variety of social pathologies (including alcoholism, incest, misogyny, violence) and risky practices (needle "sharing," unprotected sex, strolling the Leith Walk at the wrong time of night) create a Hieronymous Bosch-like effect somewhat muted in the opening section's shooting-up scene, where it is offset by realism, but horrifically present in the party scene in which Mark walks into a bedroom "whair this guy's licking oot this lassie, aboot three feet away fae whair some junkies are usin" (238). Images of helplessness also abound: Venters terminally ill (soon murdered) in his hospice bed; Spud in prison or tied up by the sadistic Laura McEwan, Mark under "House Arrest," Leslie on life support. Tommy, Wee Goagsie, David Mitchell and his girlfriend HIV-positive. Lesley's baby, Wee Dawn, and Anne Diamond's, both dead in their cribs. Kelly doesn't have a baby, she's had an abortion. Sharon is pregnant, single, and without either support or prospects. Nina's and Mark's uncle Andy dies suddenly of a heart attack, as does twenty nine year old Phil Grant. Matty, twenty five, dies of taxoplasmosis; Julie Mathieson dies of AIDS, leaving her baby an orphan (Julie is one of the novel's dead mothers to go with all the dead, and deadbeat, fathers); Mark's mentally and physically handicapped younger brother Davie dies about a year before the time of the novel, Mark's older brother Billy is killed while on duty in Northern Ireland; Dennis Ross dies after injecting himself with whiskey. "Wonder whae's next?" Spud asks after Matty's funeral. "Renton shrugged. — At least we'll be prepared, whaeivir the fuck it is," even if twelve hours drinking and pontificating . . . did little to illuminate the cruel puzzle of it all. They were no wiser now than at the start" (298–99).

At least some of the characters are a bit more knowing about another piece of the cruel puzzle of life in Leith. This is the hyper- or pathological masculinity which, while by no means a uniquely Scottish phenomenon, is nonetheless particularly noticeable in *Trainspotting*, a novel whose publication was sandwiched between two especially bloody hymns to Scottish manhood, *Rob Roy* and the even more egregious (and insidious) *Braveheart*. Welsh's novel is often cited as a prime example of "the recent spate of laddism in the arts" and the sign that "that male misogyny is alive, kicking, and applauded throughout England" (Kenyon, 1995). It is tempting, and not altogether wrong, to see *Trainspotting* in this way, as belonging to the "men-behaving-badly genre," arriving just as sales of laddie magazines such as *Loaded* spiked, and "arranged as a series of adventures that postpone adulthood," "Peter Pan in Leith" (Adams). Or worse: part of the New Bastard culture, as Pat Kane calls it, which glorifies the male violence which is itself a response to the feminization of work — or in the case of *Trainspotting*, the near absence of work of any (legal) kind and of meaningful employment in particular. (Gav Termperley works as a clerk in a district employment office, Kelly as a bartender and waitress, Billy as a soldier; otherwise the only characters with jobs exist on the periphery of the action: a policeman here, a doctor, judge, nurse, or counselor there—nothing more.) Rather than see the novel as part of the New Bastard culture, we would do better to value it for its examination of "the underlying patterns of violence and abuse" that result when the work by which men have traditionally defined themselves disappears and is replaced by "pathological manifestations of masculinity" (Whyte, 1998, 282). These include everything from alcohol abuse to violence, with women often being made to bear much of the burden. (In one characteristically illuminating yet brief, almost offhand passage, Nina realizes that the look on her cousin Geoff's face is not one of hate, as she first thought, but of drink-fueled lust, although the difference between the two may not be as great as Nina thinks.) It is easy to fault Welsh for focusing on Mark, Spud, Begbie, and Sick Boy (the last two representing the new lad at his most pathological and perverse) and miss the fact that the novel deals with its female characters both extensively and significantly. Several of them are victims of domestic abuse, others are single mothers, some are addicts and/or HIV-positive, at least one has been traumatized by incest, one actually stands up for the man who beats her, but most are well aware of the shortcomings of the men around them and angry about those shortcomings and the overall male fear of intimacy.

One way this fear manifests itself is in the way the men cultivate their hard man image by mistreating women. Related to this is the rampant homophobia that the novel exposes as one of the male characters' several "psychic defenses." Instead of pathologizing gays the way *Braveheart* does, *Trainspotting* pathologizes homophobia. This is a subject to which Welsh has returned several times, most recently and hilariously in "Catholic Guilt (You Know You Love It)," in which a homophobe dies while having sex with the twin sister of his best mate. He then discovers that the way he will be punished for the sin of homophobia is this: he will be forced to bugger any number of men until—an angel tells him—"you start to enjoy it" and "cease to feel the guilt," which he does, so much so that he pretends he doesn't just so he can continue to enjoy this form of correction. What makes Welsh's treatment of homophobia and misogyny so interesting is not just its being so rare in Scottish literature but its being connected to the novel's political context. As Whyte points out, "In a context such as Scotland's, where national self-determination continues to be a burning issue, gender antagonisms may be aggravated rather than resolved" (1998, 284). *Trainspotting* does not resolve these antagonisms; rather, it makes readers as aware of the baleful effects of hypermasculinity as Mark is when he recognizes both his own complicity in the sexist prank played on Kelly in "The Elusive Mr Hunt" and her resulting discomfort. More importantly, he realizes not only that the prank is not funny but that the men's merriment is in fact a form of "lynch mob laughter."

Even more than Mark's contemplating sex with the Italian waiter Giovanni as an acceptable alternative to the loneliness he feels in London, and indeed, throughout the novel, Alison and Kelly's meeting with the two Aussie lassies who turn out to be New Zealand lesbians suggests the liberating effects of same sex relationships as an alternative to the novel's deadening round of unsatisfying and often exploitative heterosexual relationships. Indeed, the novel carnivalizes those heterosexual relationships via the decrowning double of the four women's comical slagging off men. The women take the men's parts, impersonating their voices and biases, in a wholly if briefly devolved sexual politics with, fortunately enough, the good-natured Mark playing the fool, which is to say the man. (For a lengthier version of this same reversal, see "When the Debris Meets the Sea" in *The Acid House*.) That this devolution of women's sexual politics occurs in the section "Feeling Free" which immediately precedes "The Elusive Mr Hunt" not only underscores the novel's sexual theme; it also suggests how fragile that freedom is in *Trainspotting*'s pre-Ecstasy *mise-en-abime* of power relationships. As

Begbie and Sick Boy already know, and as David Mitchell learns in his dealings with the terminally ill Alan Venters, power is to be savored, impotence to be taken advantage of. Given that fact, might we not hear in Alison's cry, heard early in the novel, "That [heroin] beats any meat injection . . . that beats any fuckin cock in the world," the allure of heroin in a world of unsatisfying sexual relations so debased by power and male fear of intimacy.

Misogyny and homophobia are important parts of a larger social failure that led one reviewer to claim that Welsh's novel is not so much about drugs as it is about "the disillusionment of a generation." The failure and disillusionment are implied in the novel's seemingly irrelevant title. Welsh's allusion to "the compulsive British hobby of collecting locomotive numbers from the national railway system" is generally read, when read at all, as "a metaphor for shooting heroin and the obsessional, senseless nature of the addict's life" (Cardullo, 1997, 159) and "the pointlessness of drug addiction" (Kerr, 1996). Both trainspotting and heroin addiction are arbitrary ways "to give your pointless life structure" (Welsh qtd. in Leland, 1996, 53). But trainspotting is also a synechdoche that suggests the obsessive, senseless nature of the middle class punter's life and the pointlessness of an addiction to consumer capitalism, particularly in a setting where work is either all but non-existent or demeaning (Kelly's waitressing and bartending) or coerced and self-destructive (prostitution) or parodies the entrepreneurial spirit (giro schemes, drug deals, theft) or maintains not a drug habit but the status quo (policeman, judge, jobs officer, employment clerk, security guard, soldier, minister, psychiatrist, psychologist, drugs counselor). Although with few exceptions the work is either meaningless or beside any point other than growing the economy, the inherent value of work is always assumed, at least by parents, judges, and other guardians of the status quo. Of course, none of *Trainspotting*'s characters actually trainspots, least of all in Leith Central Station, then empty for thirty years—as empty as the values of Nina's, Dianne's, and Mark's parents. Mark's mother, now off the Valium she began taking after her youngest child's death, tarts herself up to the amusement of her unsympathetic neighbors; Mark's father watches the telly and advises his son to get a job. Both parents identify Sick Boy as an example of "conspicuous success," think of Begbie as a model of Scottish manhood, and are delighted when Billy proves his manhood by getting Sharon pregnant, remaining blissfully ignorant of his having abused her. Not that Sharon is to blame, either for getting pregnant or coming on to Mark right after Billy's death, hoping "she can substitute one brar fir the other"; "She was caught in this git-a-man, git-a-bairn, git-a-hoose shite that lassies git drummed intae them, and hud nae real chance ay defining hersel ootside ay they mashed-tattie-fir-brains terms ay reference" (220). Significantly, just as there are no friends among addicts, just associates and acquaintances, so there is no sense of community in the novel, other than in debased forms: sectarianism, racism, sexism, dysfunctional families, "mind-numbing" mass media (television shows and tabloid newspapers) and the like.

3

The Novel's Reception and Fallout

As the previous chapter suggests, *Trainspotting*'s critical success came to rest on the issues first raised by Glaswegian writer Jeff Torrington in a lengthy blurb that accompanied the original Secker & Warburg edition. Drastically shortened for later editions and eventually dropped altogether, Torrington's remarks not only gave a Whitbread-winning Scottish writer's imprimatur to Welsh's work; it also directed reviewers to the work's most important stylistic and thematic features:

Trainspotting marks the capital debut of a capital writer. A heavyweight champ of the vernacular, Irvine Welsh, using a bare-knuckled prose style, mounts ferocious attacks on the body state. A wickedly funny, yet irredeemably sad book, its author (what a mimetic gift the man has for gutter patois and junkie jargon!) takes us on a Hell tour of those psychic ghettos which are the stamping grounds for junkies, boozers, no hopers and losers. This marvellous novel might feel like a bad day in Bedlam, but boy is it exhilarating. Yes, it truly is!

Even as they drew on his insights, reviewers pointed to a number of features that Torrington had either missed or chosen to overlook, most notably the novel's structure and the very effective way it combines authorial detachment and "shockingly close emotional engagement" (Turner, 1996).

Although *Trainspotting* was a critical success from the start (in the Oxbridge-dominated broadsheets and literary reviews that Welsh claims to loathe), its commercial success took a bit longer to develop. As Welsh has noted, "It was only when clubby types started buying *The Acid House*, then backtracked into *Trainspotting*, that it started to shift from the shelves" ("Introduction," *Acid*, vii). First published in he summer of 1993 in a print run of 3,000 copies, *Trainspotting* had sold 50,000 by early 1995 and three times that number a year later, after having been reprinted sixteen times. By then two editions were appearing on the bestseller lists simultaneously (the regular and the film tie-in). Forced to contend with the growing number of copies of the British editions brought to the United States by club-bers, Welsh's American publisher, Norton, decided to release its edition a few weeks before the scheduled date which was to coincide with the film's opening in July. (In the United States, reviews of the book often mentioned the film and were accompanied by shots from the film, thus creating a linkage between the two forms that had not occurred in the UK.) By then, "the best book ever written by man or woman" (*Rebel Inc*) had become "the fastest-selling and most shop-lifted novel in British publishing history" (Arlidge, 1996), with sales (in and out of the UK) totaling half a million copies and still growing. Copies of the small number of hardbound copies of the first edition intended for sale to libraries, meanwhile, were fetch-ing up to £1,000 on the rare book market. By decade's end, the "courageous first novel" that had made the *Guardian*'s "Best Fiction of the Year" list in 1993 and that had been nominated for both the Booker and the Whitbread, was showing up on many of the end-of-the-millennium lists such as the *Times*' "Favourite Books of the 90s" (#5) and Waterstone's "100 Books of the Twentieth Century"

(#10) as well as in surveys of university students, who generally ranked *Trainspotting* just after Tolkien's *Lord of the Rings*.

Another measure of *Trainspotting*'s success and significance is its and Welsh's having become cultural touchstones. Reviewers busied themselves identifying the "next Irvine Welsh," the female Irvine Welsh, the English Irvine Welsh, the Welsh Irvine Welsh and Welsh's rural counterpart; writers were judged according to the Welsh standard: as good as Welsh (or not as good), in the tradition of Welsh, half Welsh or not Welsh. "Trainspotting" became part of the general cultural vocabulary and *Trainspotting* an identifiable feature of the urban landscape. There were cartoons and, of course, parodies: "Gritty Scottish Irvine Welsh follows up his bestselling expose of drug culture *Trainspotting* with a hard-hitting new novel *Pottyspotting*. It's a devastating critique of Glasgow's under-two population" (C. Brown, 1996).

Trainspotting's influence manifested itself in much more important ways. Its success focussed attention on the Scottish literary scene, its younger writers in particular. One result was the proliferation of anthologies "celebrat[ing] the extraordinary boom taking place in Scottish literature" as well as in other Welsh-related areas: youth and drugs. *Trainspotting* focussed attention on Edinburgh too, emphasizing, as an article in the *New York Times Magazine*'s "Sophisticated Traveller" supplement put it, "a side . . . that most guidebooks prefer to bypass," as did the city's tourist office. Indeed, some found Welsh's depiction "as dangerously delimiting as historical tartanry or the kailyard ever were" (Boddy, 1996 361). Others felt the same way about Welsh's "pervasive influence," which they believed "has so warped the Scottish literary scene" (Taylor, 1999). Welsh's most direct influence on Scottish politics drew a similarly outraged response. Unlike *Braveheart*, which the Scottish National Party appropriated "as a whole into its party rhetoric and images of the film into its party literature," *Trainspotting* was appropriated only by the SNP's youth wing, the Young Scottish Nationalists, for a leaflet entitled *Toryspotting*, which quoted Renton's anti-English rant and which was quickly branded "racist" (McArthur, 1998).

More broadly, *Trainspotting*'s success brought about a sea change (or yet another sea change) in British fiction, away from "being sleepy and provincial" and towards "cosmopolitan cool" and "chemical squalor" (Amidon), prompting more than one reviewer to complain of bookshelves groaning under the weight of so many Welsh "read-alikes" even as Welsh's editor rejected the vast majority of the twenty-odd Welsh-like manuscripts he received each month. One North London bookstore devoted an entire section to books endorsed by Welsh while Britain's biggest bookseller, Waterstone's, demanded that the publisher remove Welsh's endorsement from the cover of John King's *The Football Factory* — "buy, steal, or borrow a copy" — because so many readers were doing the second.

Back in Scotland, *Trainspotting* was at the center of another controversy after being selected as an approved text for the Higher English paper. A Scottish Arts Council decision to use money from the National Lottery to buy books by contemporary Scottish authors (including *Trainspotting*) drew much the same negative response from those who bemoaned this abandonment of Scottish education's commitment "to improve and elevate." To such howls of protest on the part of latterday Miss Jean Brodies to the prospect of *Trainspotting* supplanting *Treasure Island*, one commentator waggishly responded, "What is the world coming to when a novel about drug abuse gains ground over a novel about theft and treachery, drunkenness and murder?" (Home, 1996).

Those who objected to *Trainspotting* as an approved text because it failed to elevate its readers were, in a way, on to something. This is its author's aggressively anti-art aesthetic which involves the desacralization of art and refusal to affirm those values upon which the liberal humanist faith in high art (Matthew Arnold's "culture") rests.

As Nicholas Williams has explained, Welsh's work is based upon an "aesthetics of authenticity [that] takes the form of an anti-aesthetic, the evacuating of any lingering high-art appreciation in favour of the raw substance of the thing itself." The fact that Welsh does not fetishize originality but instead welcomes adaptation and remixing ("The more transformation the better" [Macdonald], 1996) further contributes to this "break-down in the concept of literature, and in cultural authority generally" (Sinfield, 1997, xv).

Once he had reached his intended audience (who were as likely to buy his books in a Virgin Megastore as a Waterstone's or W. H. Smith's), Welsh was understandably dismissive of those middle class voyeurs whom he was sometimes accused of pandering to for indulging their "addiction to addiction-watching" (Kauffmann, 1996). Taken to task by Will Self, for example, Welsh replied in kind: "I understand he's a middle class Oxbridge writer, accusing me of drug voyeurism. What the fuck is he doing reading the book [*Trainspotting*] anyway? It's not written for the Will Selfs and the other public school types of this world to pontificate over in their drawing rooms and their broadsheet columns" (Berman, 1996, 58). Admittedly, Welsh's intentions and Robertson's missionary zeal notwithstanding, publishers and booksellers that organized club readings and club tours were mainly interested in profit. But for many young readers, turned off by the work of university-trained writers who seemed to dominate the pre-Welsh literary scene, *Trainspotting* had a different attraction, one that Carol Gow, writing in *Times Higher Education Supplement*, believed should be taken seriously. Arguing that Welsh's novel should be judged according to the latitude allowed any creative text, she explains *Trainspotting*'s appeal and importance in relation to the failure of the government's "just say no" anti-drug campaign. What the novel does, Gow notes, is explore "in graphic detail why young people want to take drugs, how they take drugs and what it does to them," providing along the way "a profoundly anti-drug message without shirking from showing what attracts [its main character] to drugs." After noting how unusual it was for the paper to use its editorial space to comment on a work of fiction, the *Scotsman on Sunday* made much the same point: "In *Trainspotting*, Irvine Welsh writes about [youth and drugs] without censorship or judgment. Perhaps parents and politicians — and newspapers — should adopt the same attitude" (Editorial).

The novel that grew out of Welsh's dismay over the effects of heroin use in Edinburgh and the absence of effective public response to this use and its dire consequences (HIV infection in particular) resulted in a very useful and long overdue examination of the drug situation in Edinburgh, in the rest of Scotland and in all of Britain. The interest generated a long list of books on the subject, starting with Rebel Inc.'s publication of Kevin Williamson's *Drugs and the Party Line*, with an introduction by Welsh, and more importantly articles in the popular press that avoided the usual tone of moral panic, most notably those written by John Arlidge and published in the *Independent* from 1994 on. Welsh's own position on drug use is complex but consistent. For him heroin use is understandable (in light of the limited opportunities open to the people his characters represent) but misguided (in that heroin is a profoundly "anti-social drug," unlike ecstasy) (Farquarson, 1993). Drug use, Welsh contends, is a social issue and should be seen and dealt with as such and not as a moral matter. Looking ahead, Welsh says, he "would genuinely like to see a drug-free society. But that would mean having a lot of social and psychological needs met. That's a long way off." It is certainly far removed from the situation in *Trainspotting*, which Welsh rightly claims is not really a drug novel, but instead a novel about a drug society which focuses on a particular segment of that society at a particular moment of time, just as "the drugs of choice for many people changed from the state sponsored poisons of alcohol and tobacco to 'private sector' drugs such as heroin, then ecstasy and cocaine" (Welsh, "Drugs," 2).

· **4**

Adaptations of the Novel

Few works have come to exist in so many forms in so short a period and with such critical and commercial success: book, play, film. Harry Gibson's stage adaptation began as a radio play for the BBC; "Then they saw it," Gibson dryly noted. Theater allowed Gibson (himself a playwright) greater freedom than radio, or film, with its rating system serving as *de facto* censor. This is not to say that Gibson's adaptation was, or could be, entirely faithful to Welsh's scabrous and complex novel. Partly this was a matter of necessity. Although surprisingly faithful to Welsh's dialogue interior monologue presentation, and range of characters and narrative lines, Gibson reduced the novel's forty-three vignettes to twenty short scenes, used just four actors to play twelve parts and significantly reduced the novel's humor in order to emphasize the unrelieved grimness and futility of the characters' lives. Of course, to speak of the play as if it were a single entity is misleading. Like the novel with its several editions, each with its own paratextual terms of reference (pre- and post-film, with skull masks or with photos of the film's stars on the cover, blurbs and other orienting materials, etc.), the play exists in multiple forms, in at least two versions (only one of which has been published) and in numerous productions, from its premiere at Glasgow's Citizens Theatre as part of Mayfest and later the Traverse, to Edinburgh Festival, London, touring company and numerous stagings outside the UK, including the "sanitized version" that appeared off-Broadway in 1998 with no injecting, no body fluids, and no overflowing toilet. The two London productions of 1995 received the most attention. The first, at the Bush, directed by Ian Brown (who had also directed the Mayfest production) drew especially enthusiastic reviews. The second, staged at the Ambassador's and directed by Gibson, was not as well received, particularly by those who, having seen the earlier version, preferred both Brown's direction and the greater intimacy and resulting intensity of the Bush, in North London, to the much larger Ambassador's in the city's West End. Plus, as one reviewer noted, "There is a danger, which this production hovers just the right side of, that once it loses the raw desperation and initial shock value, it could become too fashionable and slick for its own good" (Hemming, 1995). With the release of the film version just two months away, Hemming's caveat seemed especially prophetic.

In much the same way that Welsh just signed over stage rights to Gibson and let him do what he wanted (ending up pleased with the result, especially with its attracting a young, less middle and upper middle class audience), Welsh signed over film rights to Andrew MacDonald, John Hodge and Danny Boyle, giving them similarly free rein. As MacDonald later said, Welsh "has this total belief in the house and club culture. He let us do what we wanted. He saw it like it was being remixed for an Ibiza Special or something" (Crampton, 1996, 19). Whether or not Welsh (who had a cameo as the Muirhouse dealer, Forrester) was quite as pleased with the result—a film that went on to become a commercial success and that has often been cited as all but singlehandedly reviving the moribund British and Scottish film industries—is less clear. What is clear is the speed and relative ease with which Welsh's novel went from page to screen. MacDonald first read *Trainspotting* in December 1993; two months later he gave it to Hodge, a medical doctor turned screenplay writer with whom he and director Danny Boyle had worked on *Shallow Grave*. Hodge's screenplay was ready the following December; the seven week shoot began on 22 May and the film released in the UK on 23 February 1996. (The fact that that was also the release date of Emma Thomson's heritage film version of Jane Austen's *Sense and Sensibility* led Martin Wroe, in a newspaper article cleverly titled "Hard Drugs and Heroine Addiction," to divide the British cinema audience into "trainspotters and Janespotters.")

UK distributor Polygram's surprisingly large publicity budget for this low-budget Channel Four film—fully fifty percent (not the usual ten) of the production cost (£1.7 million)—paid off handsomely. *Trainspotting* went on to become the most successful British film of 1996 on its way to earning $72 million worldwide. That may be only a tenth of what the major studio blockbuster *Independence Day* earned and less than half of *Pulp Fiction*'s worldwide box office but still about five times what successful indies *Kids* and *Shallow Grave* made. Polls in Britain listed *Trainspotting* among the top 10 British films (#3) and the "top 100 films ever" (#25). In the United States, Miramax built on its successful promotion of *Pulp Fiction* and *The Usual Suspects* to make *Trainspotting* (redubbed for the American audience) the biggest independent release of the year, with "marketing hype so high that one can hardly see the film for the magazine covers" (Taubin, 1996). And not just magazine covers. *Trainspotting* was now a novel, a play, a film, a soundtrack (double platinum, plus spinoff comprising "music from the film and more," i.e., *not* from the film), spoken-word cassette, posters, tee-shirts (#s 1–5, 8 and 24 on the HMV tee-shirt chart). By November there was also a boxed-set that included video, eight deleted scenes, interviews, sunglasses and lighter. But most of all, *Trainspotting* was "an attitude" (Champion, 1997, xiv) and a style, especially in advertising, used to market everything from the musical on rollerskates *Starlight Express* to films, CDs, sweets, sunglasses and Netscape. The film's influence was even felt in *Elizabeth*, whose director, Shekha Kapur, choose to imitate the *Trainspotting* style.

Adapting *Trainspotting* for the screen was as daunting a task as adapting it for the stage, making the swiftness and success of both all the more remarkable. In writing the screenplay Hodge faced virtually all the problems that Gibson had and resolved most in similar fashion: reducing the number of incidents (less drastically for the film, with its rapid cutting, than for the play, with its cumbersome scene changes) while still managing to "convey some of the spirit and content of the book"; "amalgamating various characters, transfering incident and dialogue from one character to another"; and doing a few things that Gibson did not: "building some scenes around minor details from the book and making up a few things altogether" (Hodge, 1996 x). (Hodge was only partly responsible for emphasizing Dianne's role; the advertising, which featured Mark/Ewan McGregor, Spud/Ewen Bremmer, Sick Boy/Jonny Lee Miller, Begbie/Robert Carlyle, and Dianne/Kelly MacDonald — did the rest.) Perhaps the most difficult problem Hodge faced (but not Gibson) was how to translate a novel largely presented as a series of interior monologues into acceptable cinematic form. Hodge's solution — to dispense with the interior monologues altogether except for the voiceovers of Renton throughout and once each by Begbie, Tommy, Dianne, and Gav — meant not only making use of what is at best a clumsy device, but more importantly making Renton even more central to the film than he is to the novel or the play. This entailed reducing, even silencing, some of the voices clamoring to be heard even as it accentuated one of the interior monologues' most interesting but overlooked features: their being so intensely visual (Paget, 1999, 132).

Unlike the play, which was invariably seen and discussed as an adaptation (and a remarkably faithful one at that), the film—because of the size of the audience it attracted, the amount of critical attention it received, and the efficacy and influence of the film's marketing—ran the risk of supplanting Welsh's text rather than merely supplementing it. In effect the film became the novel, spoke for it, as it were, in people's minds, with a number of unfortunate results. One was the narrowing of focus to Renton and drugs. Another was the jaunty, stylish depiction of heroin addiction that many saw as an endorsement of what was described. As Neil McCormick put it, the film is like the heroin experience: "It depicts some of the harshest realities of heroin addiction, but it feels great." In addition, there was considerable lightening of the humor, intensifying of the Tarantino influence, and a greater emphasis on caricature rather than character. The result is a film in which there is an unfortunate "triumph of style over substance" (McCormick, 1996) as the filmmakers make their presence felt in every scene via stylistic flourishes and intertextual references, while turning Welsh's harrowing as well as blackly humorous novel of a depressingly atomized society into another slick "buddy movie" from the makers of *Shallow Grave*. Far from duplicating the novel's sense of futility and immediacy, the film's high-speed pace—established in the opening sequence and abetted throughout by the music soundtrack—create a sense of energy and exhilaration that propels the narrative ahead. While this left some gasping in admiration, others complained that the film "sanitized" Welsh's novel, offered "the Martha Stewart version," a day at the beach rather than a guided tour of the characters' own private postindustrial hell, and therefore something on the order of the "jocular stories" Mark tells Dianne "about Spud and Begbie, sanitising them tastefully." Or, if not sanitized, then Americanized (which may be the same thing). For all its indie feel, self-consciously retro Richard Lester-Beatles movie look, and Scottish subject and vernacular, Boyle's film is, if not quite the "shrewdly calculated and commercial piece of work" that *New York* magazine disparagingly described, then certainly a work whose roots are no less in Tarantino's *Pulp Fiction* and Scorsese's *Goodfellas* as they are in Welsh's novel. And therein lies either the film's greatest weakness or its greatest triumph: its "forg[ing] a new sophisticated urban aesthetic, the combination of young cast, edgy subject matter, vibrant colours, visual pyrotechnics and a pounding soundtrack a direct allusion to the pleasures of club culture" (Petrie, 2000, 196).

It was to such pleasures—whether of heroin or of Ecstasy—that politicians objected, playing to the gallery of voters: Bob Dole and Bill Clinton in the US, Donald Dewar in the UK. Equally influential, albeit in a different way, were the views of two prominently placed writers: the Oxbridge educated addict-in-residence Will Self in the UK and the *New York Times* chief book reviewer Michiko Kakutani in the United States. Writing in the *Independent*, Self praised Welsh's novel (although he later admitted he never finished it) but blasted the film—"an extended pop video," an example of "recent drug pornography" and "a meretricious adaptation of an important book"—for being false to the experience it pretends to depict. And then he went on to blast Welsh too, for giving his *de facto imprimatur* to the film by briefly appearing in it as a drug dealer when, Self went on to say (a bit inconsistently), he doubted that Welsh had ever had "an injecting drug habit" or ever been anything more than a drug voyeur. How much of Self's criticism was based on legitimate concerns about the film and how much his more-drugged-than-thou attitude had to do with his having lost his literary addict-in-residence position to Welsh is impossible to say. What can be said with certainty is that the voyeurism issue resurfaced just a few weeks later across the Atlantic in another influential forum, the *New York Times Magazine*. Rather than attacking the film as "a meretricious adaptation of an important book" and the author as a lying profiteer, as Self had done, Kakutani lashed out at both film and novel with the kind of fervor usually associated with the far right in the ongoing culture wars. The musical *Rent*, the 1995 film *Kids*, Welsh's "nasty first novel" ("an ugly book that plays to our worst fears about youth culture") and the Boyle film made in MTV's image "are just the latest offerings from a thriving brand of tourism that offers bourgeois audiences a voyeuristic peep at an alien subculture and lets them go home feeling smug and with it."

For Alan Sinfield the translation of *Trainspotting* from subcultural novel to mainstream film offers two important lessons. One is general and concerns late-capitalism's ability to contain, absorb, and profit from dissent. The other is specific and highlights the very different politics of the two texts, especially in the film's suppressing the racism, sexism, domestic violence, and sectarian conflict, as well as the significant contrast between Mark Renton and the more Thatcher-ish Sick Boy. Equally troubling is the way the film "solves" the novel's AIDS problem by a sleight of acronymic wits, substituting MTV style for HIV substance. The downside of the film's ambiguous commercial success is most distressingly obvious in a book that studiously, even ludicrously avoids even mentioning Welsh or *Trainspotting* in any of its several forms. This is *Creative Britain*, by Chris Smith, Secretary of State for Culture, Media and Sport, pejoratively referred to as the Ministry of Fun and formerly known as the Ministry of Culture. Smith's self-serving, depressingly cliched and frighteningly bland collection of addresses on the current state of British culture focuses on four areas: "*access, excellence, education,* and *economics,*" though it is clear that it is only the last that really matters. The other three are merely the means to Smith's and the Blair government's pounds and pence approach to culture, or rather what that government prefers to call Britain's "creative industries" (music, publishing, art, radio and television, film, advertising, etc.). Thus, by a process not unlike the one described above does an Orwellian sleight of words transform the term "culture industry" coined by Theodor Adorno and Max Horkheimer in their critique of cultural commodification into its opposite as well as the means for explaining what it patently excludes as Smith burnishes the image of Cool Britannia and its revitalized film industry with *Beans* and *Bravehearts* and *Mrs. Browns* and the Ewan MacGregor of *Star Wars: The Phantom Menace.*

That exclusion may be taken as the sign that even as *Trainspotting* was being offered by paperback book clubs and *Filth*, amazingly enough, made a "Holiday Best Bet" from Book-of-the-Month Club and its softcover spinoff, Quality Paperback Book Club, Welsh was able to retain at least some of his power to disturb and was able to keep at least one foot out of the "creative industries" that had worked to his financial advantage as he had worked to theirs. Welsh is clearly resigned to, but certainly not reducible to, the uses to which his work has been put. He has noted that once a book is published and more especially once a film is released, it in effect becomes everybody's, becomes, that is, "commonly owned." There is more to Welsh's situation, indeed, his dilemma, than that, however. As Jonathan Coe noted as early as March 1994, "the rush to confer historical respectability" on Welsh, Kelman, *et al.* was part of an effort "to make 'dangerous' writing safe by finding it a comfortable niche in the literary canon" and, one might add, on the bookshelves of Waterstone's and in the warehouses of amazon.com. Perhaps the two most important effects of this conferral are these. One is that Welsh has been forced to up the violence and vulgarity quotient with each new work. The other is our tendency to forget that, as Jonathan Romney has pointed out, it is not "Welsh's fault that his book struck a vein of national zeitgeist" or that his work has been used to advance a "Cool Britannia" and "creative industries" ethos "to which Welsh's stories and style stand in bristling opposition." And that includes the tendency to forget that, as Welsh's friend and fellow writer Duncan McLean reminds us, "in those days, to write about heroin addicts on rundown Edinburgh estates was from being the easy commercialism critics often accuse Irvine of having adopted" (xiv).

Further Reading and Discussion Questions

WORKS BY IRVINE WELSH

Books

The Acid House. London: Jonathan Cape, 1994; New York: W. W. Norton, 1995.

The Acid House: A Screenplay. London: Methuen, 1999. Introduction vii–xii.

Ecstasy. London: Jonathan Cape, 1996; New York: W. W. Norton, 1996.

Filth. London: Jonathan Cape, 1998; New York: W. W. Norton, 1998.

Glue. London: Jonathan Cape, 2001; New York: W. W. Norton, 2001.

The Irvine Welsh Omnibus. London: Secker & Warburg/Jonathan Cape, 1997.

Marabou Stork Nightmares. London: Jonathan Cape, 1995; New York: W. W. Norton, 1996.

Trainspotting. London: Martin Secker & Warburg, 1993; New York: W. W. Norton, 1996.

"Trainspotting" and "Headstate." London: Minerva, 1996.

You'll Have Had Your Hole. London: Methuen, 1998. Introduction v–ix.

Selected Other Works by Welsh

"Catholic Guilt (You Know You Love It)." In *Speaking with the Angel: Original Stories*. Ed. Nick Hornby. London: Penguin Books, 2000; New York: Riverhead Books, 2001. 185–206.

"Drugs and the Theatre, Darlings." In *"Trainspotting" and "Headstate,"* 1–10.

"A Scottish George Best of Literature." In *A Life in Pieces: Reflections on Alexander Trocchi*. Eds. Allan Campbell and Tim Niel. Edinburgh: Rebel Inc., 1997. 17–19.

"Welcome to the Working Class." *Guardian*, 13 September 1996: G2T:4.

INTERVIEWS WITH WELSH

Beckett, Andy. "Irvine Welsh: The Ecstasy and the Agony." *Guardian*, 25 July 1998: 6.

———. "Raving with an MBA." *Independent on Sunday*, 23 April 1995: Review 38

Berman, Jenifer. "Irvine Welsh." *Bomb*, Summer 1996: 56–61.

Bresnark, Robin. "Irvine Welsh." *Melody Maker*, 16 January 1999: 12.

Leland, John. "Track Stars." *Newsweek*, 15 July 1996: 52–54.

Macdonald, Kevin. "Postcards from the Edge." *Independent on Sunday*, 28 January 1996: Arts 18.

McGavin, Patrick Z. " 'Trainspotting' Author 'Stumbled into Writing.' " *Chicago Tribune*, 30 July 1996: 52.

Mulholland, John. Interview with Welsh. *Guardian*, 30 March 1995: T8.

Redhead, Steve. *Repetitive Beat Generation*. Edinburgh: Rebel Inc., 2000, 137–150.

Reynolds, Simon. "Angel with a Dirty Mind: An Interview with Irving Welsh." *VLS (Village Voice* Literary Supplement), 15 September 1998: 8–11, 127.

Riddell, Mary. "The NS Interview." *New Statesman and Society*, 3 May 1999: 22–23.

Smith, Casper Llewellyn. "The Credible Voice of Rave Culture." *Daily Telegraph*, 22 April 1995.

Smith, L. C. "Welcome to the Acid House." *Spin*, August 1996: 22.

REVIEWS, ESSAYS, AND BOOKS

Adams, Tim. "Peter Panned." *Observer*, 7 December 1997: 30.

Adamson, Joseph, and Hilary Clark, eds. *Scenes of Shame: Psychoanalysis, Shame, and Writing*. Albany: State U of New York Press, 1999.

Alvarez, Maria. "Return of the Culture Club." *Sunday Times*, 9 June 1996: Style 14.

Arlidge, John. "Return of the Angry Young Men." *Observer*, 23 June 1996: 14.

Bahr, David. "After 'Trainspotting,' a Truer, Darker Comic Vision." *New York Times*, 15 August 2000: 2:25.

Baker, John F. "Short Takes." *Publishers Weekly*, 15 January 2001: 16.

Bakhtin, Mikhail. *Rabelais and His World*. Trans. Helene Iswolsky. Bloomington: Indiana UP, 1984.

"Bard of the Scheme Scene." *Bookseller*. 12 May 1995: 28–29.

Bell, Ian. Rev. of *Trainspotting*. *Observer*, 15 August 1993: 47.

Bell, Ian A. "Imagine Living There: Form and Ideology in Contemporary Scottish Fiction." In *The Regional Novel in Britain and Ireland*. Ed. K. D. M. Snell. Cambridge: Cambridge UP, 1998. 217–233.

Boddy, Kasia. "Scotland." *The Oxford Guide to Contemporary Writing*. Ed. John Sturrock. New York: Oxford UP, 1996. 361–376.

Brooks, Xan. *Choose Life: Ewan McGregor and the British Film Revival*. London: Chameleon Books, 1998.

Brown, Craig. "My Forecasts for 1997." *Daily Telegraph*, 21 December 1996.

Brown, Mick. "Generation." *Telegraph Magazine*, 5 July 1995.

Cardullo, Bert. "Fiction into Film, or, Bringing Welsh to a Boyle." *Literature/Film Quarterly* 25.3 (1997): 158–162.

Champion, Sarah, ed. *Disco Biscuits: New Fiction from the Chemical Generation*. London: Sceptre, 1997.

Cheever, John. *Falconer*. New York: Knopf, 1977.

Coe, Jonathan. "Where Angels Fear to Tread." *Sunday Times*, 10 March 1994: 7:13.

Cowley, Jason. "Prickly Flower of Scotland." *Times*, 13 March 1997: 33.

Craig, Cairns. *The Modern Scottish Novel: Narrative and the National Imagination*. Edinburgh: Edinburgh UP, 1999.

Crampton, Roger. "The Hit Squad." *The Times Magazine*, 20 January 1996: 18–21.

Crawford, Robert. *Devolving English Literature*, 2nd ed. Edinburgh: Edinburgh UP, 2000.

Critty, Patrick. "Prickly Thistle." *Times Literary Supplement*, 19 January 2001: 27.

Curtis, Nick. "Drug-Fuelled Romances: Scottish Fiction." *Financial Times*, 8 June 1996: 12.

"Designed to Shock." *Financial Times*, 11 March 1998: 13.

Downer, Lesley. "The Beats of Edinburgh." *New York Times Magazine*, 15 March 1996: 42–45.

Editorial. "Trainspotting's Lessons for Middle Britain." *Scotland on Sunday*, 4 February 1996.

Farquarson, Kenny. "Through the Eye of a Needle." *Scotland on Sunday*, 8 August 1993.

Freeman, Alan. "Ghosts in Sunny Leith: Irvine Welsh's *Trainspotting*." *Studies in Scottish Fiction: 1945 to the Present*. Ed. Susanne Hagemann. Frankfurt: Peter Lang, 1996. 251–262.

Gordon, Giles. "Pandering to the English View of Scotland the Drugged." *Scotsman*, 13 June 1997.

Gow, Carol. "*Trainspotting* Is Less Dangerous than Ignorance." *Times Higher Education Supplement*, 22 March 1996: 26.

Grant, Iain. "Dealing Out the Capital Punishment: Irvine Welsh." *Sunday Times*, 5 September 1993: SC14.

Gross, John. "A Fashionable Pusher of Horrid Little Buttons." *Sunday Telegraph*, 31 December 1995.

Hagemann, Susanne. Introduction. *Studies in Scottish Fiction: 1945 to the Present*. Ed. Hagemann. : Frankfurt: Peter Lang, 1996. 7–15.

Hemming, Sarah. "Grim Wit in a Drug Wasteland." *Financial Times*, 21 December 1995: 11.

Hill, John. "British Cinema as National Cinema." In Murphy 178–187.

Hodge, John. *"Trainspotting" and "Shallow Grave."* London: Faber and Faber, 1996.

Home, Colette Douglas. "48-Hour Rule That Can Give Families a Chance." *Daily Mail*, 15 November 1996: 9.

Howard, Jennifer. "Fiction in a Different Vein." *Washington Post*, 8 September 1996: Book World 1, 9.

Hughes-Hallett, Lucy. "Cruising for a Bruising." *Sunday Times*, 15 August 1993: 6:8.

"It's Generational and Geographical." *Scotsman*, 26 February 1994.

Jameson, Fredric. *Postmodernism, or, The Cultural Logic of Late Capitalism.* Durham: Duke UP, 1991.

Johnson, Daniel. "Enter the New Nihilists." *Daily Telegraph*, 7 November 1998.

Jolly, Mark. "Books in Brief." *New York Times Book Review*, 28 July 1996: 19.

Kakutani, Michiko. "Slumming." *New York Times Magazine*, 26 March 1996: 16.

Kane, Pat. "Fatal Knowledge of Inescapable Masculinity." *Scotland on Sunday*, 16 July 1995.

Kauffmann, Stanley. "Scotland Now, England Then." *New Republic*, 19 and 26 August 1996: 38–39.

Kenyon, Meb, and Phyllis Nagy. "Season of Lad Tidings." *Guardian*, 4 December 1995: 7.

Kerr, Euan. National Public Radio's *Morning Edition* 26 July 1996.

King, Chris Savage. "Voices from the Edge." *Sunday Times*, 16 April 1995: 9:13.

Kravitz, Peter, ed. *The Picador Book of Contemporary Scottish Fiction.* London: Picador, 1997.

Lasdun, James. "A Smart Cunt." *Village Voice*, 23 July 1996: 74.

Lury, Karen. "Here and Then: Space, Place and Nostalgia in British Youth Cinema of the 1990s." In Murphy 100–108.

Macaulay, Alastair. "Dramatic Shape-Ups Offstage and On." *Financial Times*, 15 March 1996: 17.

Maconie, Stuart. "Fool Britannia." *Times*, 26 December 1998: 24.

Massie, Allan. "Question: How Do You Make a Trendy Book Boring to Children?" *Daily Mail*, 11 November 1996: 8.

McArthur, Colin. "*Braveheart* and the Scottish Aesthetic Dementia." In *Screening the Past: Film and the Representation of History*. Ed. Tony Barta. Westport: Praeger, 1998. 167–187.

McCormick, Neil. "Too Much Junkie Business?" *Daily Telegraph*, 15 February 1996.

McIlvanney, Liam. "Divided We Stand: Scotlands For Ever." *Times Literary Supplement*, 21 April 2000: 25.

McKay, Ron. "Would the Real Irvine Welsh Shoot Up?" *Observer*, 4 February 1996: Review 9.

McLean, Duncan, "Time Bombs: A Short History of the Clocktower Press." *Ahead of Its Time: A Clocktower Press Anthology*. Ed. McLean. 1997; London: Vintage, 1998. ix–xvii.

Murphy, Robert, ed. *British Cinema of the 90s*. London: British Film Institute, 2000.

Paddy, David Ian. "No Future: Postmodern British Fiction at the End of the World." PhD diss. U of Maryland 1997.

Paget, Derrick. "Speaking Out: The Transformations of *Trainspotting*." In *Adaptations: From Text to Screen, Screen to Text*. Eds. Deborah Cartwell and Imelda Whelehan. London: Routledge, 1999. 128–140.

Peter, John. "Theatre Check." *Sunday Times*, 9 April 1995: 10:52.

Petrie, Duncan. *Screening Scotland*. London: British Film Institute, 2000.

Porlock, Harvey. "Boyfriend? Wet Patch?" *Sunday Times*, 9 June 1996: 7:2.

Reynolds, Simon. "High Society." *Artforum*, Summer 1996: 15–17.

Riddell, Mary. "The NS Interview." *New Statesman and Society*, 3 May 1999: 22–23.

Ritchie, Harry, ed. *Acid Plaid: New Scottish Writing*. London: Bloomsbury, 1996.

Roberts, Rex. "Is It Ecstasy or Existentialism?" *Insight on the News*, 16 September 1996: 34.

Romero, Dennis. "Adding a Little Grit to Modern Novels." *Los Angeles Times*, 26 June 1996: E1, E8.

Romney, Jonathan. "The Acid House, Bleak House." *Guardian*, 1 January 1999: Friday 6.

Royle, Nicholas, ed. *A Book of Two Halves: New Football Short Stories*. London: Gollancz, 1996.

Self, Will. "Carry On Up the Hypodermic." *Observer*, 11 February 1996: 6.

Sinfield, Alan. *Literature, Politics and Culture in Postwar Britain*. London: Athlone P, 1997.

Skinner, John. "Contemporary Scottish Novelists and the Stepmother Tongue." In *English Literature and Other Languages*. Eds. Ton Hoenselaars and Marius Buning. Amsterdam: Rodopi, 1999. 211–220.

Smith, Andrew. "Irvine Changes Trains." *Sunday Times*, 1 February 1998: Culture 6.

Smith, Chris. *Creative Britain*. London: Faber and Faber, 1998.

Smith, Murray. "Transnational Trainspotting." In *The Media in Britain: Current Debates and Developments*. Eds. Murray Smith, Jane Stokes, and Anna Reading. London: Macmillan, 1999. 219–227.

Spencer, Charles. "Nightmare City." *Daily Telegraph*, 4 April 1995.

Stevenson, Randall, and Gavin Wallace, eds. *Scottish Theatre Since the Seventies*. Edinburgh: Edinburgh UP, 1996.

Taubin, Amy. "Making Tracks." *Village Voice*, 23 July 1996: 66.

Taylor, Alan. "My Kind of Century." *Scotland on Sunday*, 21 February 1999: 7:12.

Thomas, Richard, ed. *Vox 'n' Roll: Hot Sauce with Everything*. London: Serpent's Tail, 2000.

Turner, Jenny. "Love's Chemistry." *Guardian*, 31 May 1996: G2T:17.

———. "Sick Boys." *London Review of Books*, 2 December 1993: 10.

Wallace, Gavin. "Voices in Empty Houses: The Novel of Damaged Identity." In Wallace and Stevenson 217–231.

Wallace, Gavin, and Randall Stevenson, eds. *The Scottish Novel Since the Seventies*. Edinburgh: Edinburgh UP, 1993.

Walsh, John. "The Not-So-Shady Past of Irvine Welsh." *Independent* 15 April 1995: Weekend 25.

Walsh, Maeve. "It Was Five Years Ago Today." *Independent on Sunday*, 21 March 1999.

Whyte, Christopher. "Masculinities in Contemporary Scottish Fiction." *Forum for Modern Language Studies*, 34.3 (1998): 274–285.

Whyte, Hamish, and Janice Galloway, eds. *Scream, If You Want to Go Faster: New Writing Scotland No. 9.* Aberdeen: Association for Scottish Literary Studies, [1991].

Williams, Nicholas M. "The Dialect of Authenticity: The Case of Irvine Welsh's *Trainspotting.*" In *English Literature and Other Languages.* Eds. Ton Hoenselaars and Marius Bunig. Amsterdam: Rodopi, 1999. 221–230.

Williamson, Kevin, ed. *Children of Albion Rovers.* Edinburgh: Rebel Inc., 1997.

Wroe, Martin, "Hard Drugs and Heroine Addiction." *Observer*, 10 March 1996: 13.

Young, Elizabeth. "Blood on the Tracks." *Guardian*, 15 August 1993: 8.

WEBSITES

www.irvinewelsh.net
www.irvinewelsh.com
www.slainte.org.uk/scotwrit/authors/welsh.htm

DISCUSSION QUESTIONS

1. *Trainspotting* has been compared to J. D. Salinger's debut novel, *Catcher in the Rye* (1951). How appropriate is the comparison?

2. How limiting or enabling do you find Welsh's use of dialect and handling of local setting?

3. Try to imagine the novel focused on one of the other "main" characters: Spud, Begbie, Tommy or Sick Boy? How would it

be different? What if it were focused on Davie Mitchell? On Kelly, Lesley or Dianne?

4. *Trainspotting* is often described as a novel about drugs. Is this an accurate description? How much of the novel concerns drugs?

5. The novel's final section is atypical in that it is narrated in the third person and in standard English. Why? What's the effect?

6. To what extent do you think that the success of *Trainspotting* and perhaps your own enjoyment of it derives from voyeurism and subcultural slumming?

7. How accurate is the novel's depiction of heroin addiction? Should we distinguish here between clinical accuracy and verisimilitude?

8. Do you find in *Trainspotting* any evidence of the sensationalism, sentimentality and didacticism that others have noticed in Welsh's later work?

9. Which do you find more powerful: the "kick" of Welsh's high-energy style of the "blow" he delivers to "the body state"?

10. Is Mark Renton's cynicism justified? Is it contagious?

11. Which *Trainspotting* do you prefer: Welsh's novel or Boyle's film?